Evangelical Landscapes

Evangelical Landscapes

Facing Critical Issues of the Day

John G. Stackhouse, Jr.

Baker Academic

A Division of Baker Book House Co
Grand Rapids, Michigan 49516

© 2002 by John G. Stackhouse, Jr.

Published by Baker Academic
a division of Baker Book House Company
P.O. Box 6287, Grand Rapids, MI 49516-6287

Printed in the United States of America

Library of Congress Cataloging-in-Publication Data

Stackhouse, John Gordon.
    Evangelical landscapes : facing critical issues of the day /
John G. Stackhouse, Jr.
        p.   cm.
    Includes bibliographical references and index.
    ISBN 0-8010-2594-X (pbk.)
    1. Evangelicalism. I. Title.
BR1640.S68 2002
270.8′3—dc21   2002066589

For information about Baker Academic, visit our web site:
www.bakeracademic.com

To
Mark
and
Marty

Contents

Preface

There are the great landscape painters: those who meticulously study a view, prepare themselves with discipline, and then render detailed and insightful representations of what they see and feel so that the rest of us can see and feel in new ways. Luminaries such as Paul Cézanne and Claude Monet can depict the same subject, even from the same vantage point, again and again, each time expanding our vision and deepening our connection with what is portrayed.

The history of North American evangelicalism has been blessed with some superb artists, especially in this last generation or so. Timothy Smith, William McLoughlin, George Marsden, Mark Noll, Nathan Hatch, Harry Stout, Edith Blumhofer, Grant Wacker, Randall Balmer, Donald Dayton—the list goes on. The portraits these scholars have rendered have helped thousands of readers to view evangelicalism in new ways—some of them profoundly new. Even the greats, however, do not see or feel all there is to see and feel. Lesser artists can make their own contributions as they interpret subjects painted by the masters.

The essays of this volume are collected from my own sketchbook, and I offer them for what understanding they might give to important subjects, several of which have already been treated by the luminaries in North American evangelical historiography. These articles are indeed essays: sweeping portrayals of large matters, offering analysis and opinion in roughly equal measure. Some are festooned with citations and notes; others bravely make their way almost bereft of academic apparatus. The objective of each one, however, is the same: both to inform and to persuade. As painters, so essayists: We do not intend to offer dispassionate data for the viewer's or reader's disinterested ingestion! We want people to see and feel differently about things that matter because they have encountered our portraits.

9

North American evangelicalism is the community-of-communities in which I have made my own religious way. I present these essays, therefore, with the love of a family member—critical, yes, but fundamentally loyal to this tradition that has tried, and often succeeded, to portray the image of Christ.

Acknowledgments

I wrote these essays with a lot of help. Student assistants at Northwestern College, the University of Manitoba, and Regent College performed invaluable service. I gladly recall the diligence and creativity of Michael Haverdink, Jena Dukes, Crystal Dykstra, Mary Massel, Patricia Janzen Loewen, and Keith Grant. Elizabeth Powell, the latest in this succession, worked with me on the preparation of this volume with cheerfulness and grace.

Scholarship requires money, and I acknowledge the support of the following agencies over the years: the Canadian Studies Program of the Canadian Embassy to the United States of America; the Social Sciences and Humanities Research Council of Canada; the Institute for the Study of American Evangelicals; and the Abilene (now Georgetown) Foundation.

Scholarship also requires time, and I affirm the board of governors, administration, and faculty of Regent College for agreeing that Regent's professors must have time for research and thus making sure that we do. I am particularly glad for a research leave in the autumn of 2001 that allowed me to compose this book.

I render thanks also to editors Robert N. Hosack and Melinda Van Engen at Baker Academic, who supported this project with both encouragement and skill.

My mentors—Mark Noll and Martin Marty—likely will recognize in these essays a few of their own brilliant ideas, categories, and provocations reflected dimly but enthusiastically in my efforts to extend their great contributions to the understanding of North American religion. To them I gratefully dedicate this book.

Finally, my beloved Kari and my treasured Trevor, Joshua, and Devon make all of my work possible because they make my life good.

Earlier versions of some of these essays appeared in print in the following locations:

"Women in Public Ministry in Twentieth-Century Canadian and American Evangelicalism: Five Models," *Studies in Religion/Sciences Religeuses* 17 (fall 1988): 471–85; "Billy Graham and the Nature of Conversion: A Paradigm Case," *Studies in Religion/Sciences Religeuses* 21 (1992): 337–50; "Perpetual Adolescence: The Emerging Culture of North American Evangelicalism," *Crux* 29 (September 1993): 32–37; "Speaking in Tongues," *Crux* 35 (December 1999): 2–12; "Faith and the Media," *Crux* 35 (March 1999): 26–32; "Money and Theology in American Evangelicalism," in *More Money, More Ministry: Money and Evangelicals in Recent American History,* ed. Larry Eskridge and Mark A. Noll (Grand Rapids: Eerdmans, 2000), 406–18; "Evangelical Theology Should Be Evangelical," in *Evangelical Futures: A Conversation on Theological Method,* ed. John G. Stackhouse, Jr. (Grand Rapids: Baker, 2000), 39–58.

1

Perpetual Adolescence

The Current Culture of North American Evangelicalism

"When I was a child, I talked like a child, I thought like a child, I reasoned like a child" (1 Cor. 13:11). This apostolic testimony ironically has been the experience of many of us in a Christian church even as adults, not just in our literal childhoods. Many of us know what it is like to think and act like a child, and to be treated like one, in a religious community. In such a community, a certain select few function as "parents." Usually they have clerical titles and credentials, but they also may be important laypeople. Sometimes they are theological professors or Bible teachers; other times they are popular authors who live far away or long ago but whose writings continue to exert unquestioned authority. These "parents" have all the status, all the knowledge, all the wisdom, and all the power. The rest of us do as we're told—if we're good children—or perhaps resist and suggest changes, acts that stigmatize us as bad children.

Life is clear, starkly clear, for "children" in such a situation. Rules govern all of life, and rewards and punishment are meted out in strict proportion to one's dutiful observance of them. Originality is not sought; creativity is feared; and initiative in any direction other than compliance with the established patterns is condemned as downright subversive. It is also true, to be sure, that in this system one always knows where one stands. At the end of each day, you can measure yourself against the parental standards, and if you've been a good boy or girl, you can rest easy—that is, at least until tomorrow morning, when you'll have to get up and behave yourself all day all over again.

This is the world of fundamentalism, of sectarianism, of certain kinds of conservative Christian religion. And, for many Christians, it is a world they are happy to have escaped. Now they don't have to kowtow to authority figures. Now they don't have to mindlessly agree and joylessly obey. Now they are free. They are free from an authoritarianism that kept them in perpetual spiritual childhood. But this freedom marks only a beginning, an opportunity. What are they free now to become and to do?

There are signs all around us that such Christians are in a state of adolescence. Adolescence is an appropriate phase to pass through, but many are not just "passing through" it. As certain Christians—even whole communities of them—have left behind the childhood of fundamentalism, many have opted for a perpetual adolescence and therefore are dangerously poised to conform completely to much of contemporary popular culture, a culture that has made a virtual cult of adolescence.

In the book *Dancing in the Dark,* a provocative study of contemporary youth culture, Quentin Schultze and his colleagues describe the emergence of the concept of adolescence.[1] At the turn of the century, American psychologist G. Stanley Hall popularized the concept of adolescence as a way of understanding the condition of young people in a state between childhood and adulthood. This transition was given a special status and a special task: Adolescents were people preparing for adulthood, and they were to do so through vigorous physical exercise, vocational as well as classical courses in high school, training in social skills, and so on.

From the 1920s onward, however, as Schultze and company point out, "adolescence became less a time to prepare for adulthood than an attempt to delay or prevent it."[2] Physical exercise became the worship of the body—from the adulation of sports heroes to the quest for a beautiful physique to the pursuit of sexual pleasure. The opening up of the curriculum to include "practical" skills gave way to a preoccupation with earn-

1. Quentin J. Schultze et al., *Dancing in the Dark: Youth, Popular Culture, and the Electronic Media* (Grand Rapids: Eerdmans, 1991).
    2. Ibid., 38.

ing money and the neglect of disciplined thought about anything other than financial success. The original concern for social skills became perverted into intricate, enslaving codes of conspicuous consumption and one-upmanship: who's in and who's out, who's hot and who's not—all based on the ephemeral qualities of good looks, big bucks, cool clothes, hot music, and the accelerating merry-go-round of fashion. And ironically, a whole new group of authority figures arose to give order and direction to this disoriented multitude: rock stars, athletes, actors, MTV producers, and columnists in youth-oriented magazines.

Perhaps the worst dimension of this process was that the legitimate concerns of adolescence—to escape from parental dominance, to discover an individual identity, and to begin an independent life—became stuck in a whirlpool of self-centered introspection and self-indulgent behavior. *I* matter most. What is good is what pleases me and helps me and stimulates me; what is bad is what annoys me or restricts me or bores me.

We aging baby boomers have made a cult of adolescence. We still want to be eighteen or perhaps twenty-five, and we have transformed popular culture around us as we always have, through the power of our numbers and our wallets. So radio stations keep playing the music of our youth—not of today's youth—even as one wonders how appropriate it is for a fifty-seven-year-old executive to be listening to hours of adolescent love songs. So jeans companies let us stay in our Levi's or khakis by bringing out "relaxed fit" pants to suit our ever more relaxed bellies and bottoms. So the ordinary necessities of the middle decades of life become glossed and airbrushed and jazzed up to let us maintain the façade of perpetual youth: Minivans are sensible for this time of life but terribly dull, so we buy impractical SUVs instead.

So now, instead of there being one generation of adolescents at a time, we have at least two! Might this trend of arrested adolescence continue indefinitely? It seems to be continuing in modern evangelical Christianity.

What's hot and what's not nowadays in the church? Music can serve as one example—a very important example for almost every churchgoer. What's hot—at least in some churches—are electric guitars, synthesizers, and vocalists backing up Scripture songs and choruses. What's not are pipe organs or pianos accompanying hymns. Is there anything wrong with that?

What's wrong with that is what's wrong with—or at least limited about—pop music in general. Except for the very best, it generally hits you hard with a shot of pleasure, and then it leaves you physically and emotionally stimulated but intellectually and spiritually malnourished. Most of it is junk food: You don't need teeth to eat it, and there is nothing to digest. The moronic "Baby, baby, love, love" of MTV gets baptized into "Jesus, Jesus, love, love" with approximately the same effect: warm fuzzies.

Now, I welcome my share of warm fuzzies, and I like a wide range of popular music. The best of it expresses basic feelings in primary—even neon—colors of the soul. The same can be said for the Christian versions of it. But Christians are not growing when their worship music is restricted to five-chord pop tunes, endlessly repeated choruses, and lyrics that—at best—contain interchangeable bits of Scripture with no obvious progression of thought. "Precious Jesus, Rock of Ages, / Holy Great I Am, / Friend of Sinners, Our Messiah, / Worthy Is the Lamb"—oh, dear! (I would now warn readers that this impressive lyric of my very own composition—indeed, composed right here on the spot—is protected by copyright *if* I believed that one could actually remember it for more than two minutes.) There is more to Christ and the Christian life than such simplicities, no matter how sincerely expressed, and other music, other worship styles in general, are needed to express this "more."[3]

What's hot also includes problem-solving sermons and therapeutic pastoring. We want sermons about us: how to be happy, how to have a happy marriage (my wife's personal teeth-grinding "favorite" was a women's group curriculum called "How to Be the Wife of a Happy Husband"), how to raise happy children happily—and, of course, the twelve steps to follow in

3. Martin E. Marty opines similarly regarding "the widely sung if not widely popular 'praise songs.' They are smooth, synthetic, unmemorable and undisturbing. They touch the sensations but not the spirit. (I'd offer an example, but for the life of me I can't think of one.) They are not made to get into the brain cells where memories disturb or quicken us" ("The Cutting Edge," *The Christian Century* [24 February 1993]: 223).

each case. Again, these are important parts of life, and pastors properly address them. But adolescents tend to exaggerate the scale of their problems and to distort reality around their own self-importance—and nothing, *nothing*, matters more than their feelings. Every crush is the Greatest Romance of All Time. Every personal setback is a crushing defeat. Nothing is more important than my relationships, my successes, my well-being, my happiness.

But what about doctrine? What about politics, and art, and literature? What about self-control, and discipline, and stewardship, and patience? What about oppression and injustice, liberation and peace—not just the healing of our own wounds and the actualization of our own potential? What about disappointment, failure, and betrayal? It is as if these things almost never cross our minds, as if they are off in another dark category somewhere marked "For Grown-ups."

Let me be clear that I am not critical of Christians who go out into popular culture and try to meet people where they are. I am not critical of Christians who hold services in their churches that are designed entirely to welcome seekers. In fact, I am supportive of efforts to make these contacts, and I frankly think we need more initiatives like them. What I am concerned about is the matter of where we go from here. Do we ever help our seeking friends progress toward spiritual depth? Or do we instead stay happily splashing in the shallows?

Another adolescent theme is the veneration of heroes. Just as popular culture has its trendsetters, its Madonnas and Michael Jordans and Steven Spielbergs, so do evangelical Christians have their authority figures: speakers such as Charles Swindoll and Josh McDowell, televangelists such as Pat Robertson and Robert Schuller, singers such as Carmen and Twila Paris, authors such as Tony Campolo and Tim LaHaye, and, perhaps above all nowadays, James Dobson. Many Christians, acting like adolescents generally, look up to all of these, it seems, without a critical thought in their heads, and once a figure has been embraced, he or she is embraced with powerful, unquestioning devotion. Wendy Kaminer, in her book on the recovery movement, *I'm Dysfunctional, You're Dysfunctional*, characterizes the discourse among such people as "instructing and witnessing. Experts, with their books, tapes, and lectures, instruct.

Group members witness (tell their stories of abuse, addiction, victimization). No one discusses. No one asks for clarification, analysis, evidence. No one inquires about the implications of a statement or challenges its validity."[4] This is a far cry from the New Testament example of the Bereans, who "examined the Scriptures every day to see if what Paul said was true" (Acts 17:11).

Adolescents typically have trouble with responsibility. Able to accomplish a great deal because of their talents and energies, they also often disappoint by dropping out of things when the novelty wears off and the demands mount up. Or when they make mistakes, damaging other people's property or feelings, they can madden with their blithe self-centeredness that sees things only in terms of their own advantage and happiness. "I promised to show up early to help with the Sunday school and then didn't show up at all? Well, I was at the mall late on Saturday night, and I must have slept in." "I held a party while my folks were away and the house got trashed? Sorry, Mom and Dad."

But adult "adolescent" evangelicals act the same way. Many of my acquaintances have worked for evangelical organizations and have been mistreated along similar lines. "Sure, we promised you that much money at the end of your summer's work with us, but we didn't have as many campers as we thought we would, so we won't pay you as much as we agreed on. After all, this is the Lord's work, right?" "Sure, we signed a contract, but things didn't go very well, and we're not going to honor it—and we know you'll understand because this is, after all, *a ministry.*" "Yes, we borrowed your equipment and put a hole through it— here it is, back again [unrepaired], sorry. (Hey, why do you look so unforgiving? I thought you were a Christian too!)"

In all of this there is the horrible weightlessness of cheap grace, a perverse detachment from responsibility. Pelagius, Erasmus, and Kant rise up from their graves and say, "Aha! We *told* you this talk of free salvation would make antinomians of you! We *told* you that people would take advantage of God's generous forgiveness! We *told* you that if people got what they

4. As paraphrased by Paul R. Fries, "Telling It (Almost) as It Is," *Perspectives* (February 1993): 20.

wanted from God without earning it they would run with it into self-indulgence!" It is not just the hypocrites on TV that embarrass evangelicalism. We encounter them in the stories of many friends who all seem to have met at least one "born-againer" who lied to them, cheated them, or otherwise sinned against them with—and this is what galls each one—this apparently impervious insouciance, this infuriating effervesence of already-forgiven bliss, this insular attitude of "I'm-cool-'cause-Jesus-loves-me-and-so-I-don't-owe-you-a-thing." This is evangelical adolescence at its most scandalous: when other people start to predict dishonesty and unreliability on the basis of how loudly one proclaims one's evangelical faith.

Schultze and his colleagues point to one final characteristic of youth culture today. Adolescents (and their baby boomer elders) know a great deal about international celebrities: The media track the lives of Britney Spears, Julia Roberts, Michael Jackson, and so on with ruthless tenacity. But we don't know much about local musicians, local artists, local politicians—or local pastors. Adolescents (and their baby boomer elders) are deeply attached to their favorite musical groups, sports teams, TV shows, and soft drinks. But we are not deeply attached to our local churches, clubs, or—in the all-too-common worst cases—families. We are lost in space and time. We are communicating with multinational media and entertainment corporations, drawing our sense of identity and purpose and meaning from them rather than from our families, neighborhoods, and churches. Indeed, adolescents typically move in and out of romances, friendships, clubs, and other relationships with little deep commitment. They are "loyal" only as long as they "like it," as if these relationships were consumer products to be purchased and discarded at will.

In the same way, contemporary evangelicalism has been fragmented a thousand ways through the proliferation of congregational, denominational, and parachurch options. Loyalty to a group, especially a local congregation and denominational tradition, is now regarded as a quaint heirloom from Grandpa and Grandma's day. We are loyal to those organizations that suit us individually, whether World Vision, *Moody Monthly*, Mennonite Central Committee, Awana Clubs, InterVarsity Christian Fellowship, and so on. And when they don't suit us any longer, we move on to another option, another "brand" or "product."

As I suggest elsewhere in this volume in greater detail, parachurch organizations cannot provide the full-fledged alternative cultures that Christian families, Christian small groups, and Christian churches can provide. Caring, ongoing, integrating Christian communities—what sociologists call "mediating structures" between the individual and the massive impersonalities of state, mass media, public education, big business, and so on—are necessary to meet the challenges of our time. When Mr. or Ms. Evangelical try to cope with a problem or succeed in an opportunity, InterVarsity and Focus on the Family and World Vision cannot talk with them in their living room, but local Christians bound to them in covenant *will* be there.

If we cannot—and would not—go back to a fundamentalist childhood and we seek to go beyond an arrested adolescence, what is the alternative? Some evangelicals have gone through fundamentalism *and* this popular style of evangelicalism and have "gotten beyond all that." Now they are (1) high church types, "into" sacramental worship and the early church, with heroes such as Robert Webber and Peter Gillquist; or (2) social action types, "into" ecology, civil rights for minorities, food for the hungry, and so on, with Ron Sider and Jim Wallis as models; or (3) feminist types, "into" moderate evangelical feminism such as that of Christians for Biblical Equality or perhaps more radical alternatives offered by Virginia Ramey Mollenkott, Rosemary Radford Ruether, or Mary Daly; or (4) spiritual types, "into" spirituality, whether strongly Christian varieties as offered by Richard Foster, Henri Nouwen, or Eugene Peterson, or more experimental sorts, such as those proffered by Thomas Moore or Joseph Campbell; or (5) intellectual types who used to love Josh McDowell and Francis Schaeffer but who now explore a wide range of theologians and philosophers, enjoying the arcana of Hermann Dooyeweerd, the massive work of Karl Barth or Hans Urs von Balthasar, the excitement of liberation theology, or the pillars of Reformation orthodoxy.

Are these concerns, each of which has enriched my life to at least some extent, in fact bad things? Again, it depends on the attitude. One must ask whether these pursuits are essentially self-centered, focused on one's own growth and satisfaction.

Are these pursuits in fact serving as grounds for conceit and, particularly, self-righteousness—the odious, false superiority of the slightly older adolescent sibling? Or do they connect Christians together in love as each brings God's gifts to the other? Do they cause us to rejoice in the diversity of the body of Christ and to strengthen one another for worship and for service to the world God loves? If these pursuits do not move us out of ourselves toward God and God's whole church and God's whole world, then we have just traded one narrow-minded, self-serving adolescent fad for another.

So what's left as an alternative? Middle age?! Many of us in our thirties—and forties!—resist the term "middle-aged," and for good reason, for the term does not mean simply the "middle age" between youth and old age. It connotes a kind of routine, a rut—a dull, ordered, monotonous, repetitive life. No new thoughts. No adventures. Just the slow, crushing press of duty and responsibility and disappointed idealism. Yecch! It seems a living death. And, to be sure, it can be just as self-centered, just as preoccupied in its own way with its own agenda, as adolescence typically is. No, growing older is not the same as growing up.

So we cannot look to middle age as a model, particularly as much evangelicalism shows many signs of middle age in its boring worship, irrelevant preaching, and ossified leadership. Let us consider a biblical word instead: *maturity*. So the apostle Paul's inspired Letter to the Ephesians:

> The gifts he [Christ] gave were that some would be apostles, some prophets, some evangelists, some pastors and teachers, to equip the saints for the work of ministry, for building up the body of Christ, until all of us come to the unity of the faith and of the knowledge of the Son of God, to maturity, to the measure of the full stature of Christ. We must no longer be children, tossed to and fro and blown about by every wind of doctrine, by people's trickery, by their craftiness in deceitful scheming. But speaking the truth in love, we must grow up in every way into him who is the head, into Christ.
>
> 4:11–15 NRSV

What are the marks of maturity? Let us focus on one, the one that Jesus himself gave when asked about spiritual completeness: "Love the Lord your God with all your heart and with all your soul and with all your mind. . . . Love your neighbor as yourself" (Matt. 22:37, 39). This is not the adolescent love of eros, the desire to acquire, the egocentric appetite. This is the love of the other for its own sake, the care for someone else's feelings and preferences and needs. This is the forgetting of self and the enjoyment of service.

If we could ask just one question with regard to each decision we make, one question that would challenge radically our bent toward selfishness and remind us of this alternative of maturity, it would be this: How can I love God and my neighbor in this situation?

Consider how this would affect the choices that all of us have to make. Choices of business partners, friends, and spouses. Choices of congregation and ongoing commitment to a particular congregation. Choices of clothing, housing, entertainment, and hobbies. Choices of political support and participation, neighborhood involvement, charities, and other ministries. How can I love God and my neighbor in this?

Consider how our churches would decide matters, not on the basis of "what suits us best" or "what we prefer" but on the basis of "what will help us worship God best, what will help us establish an authentic Christian community, and what will do the most for the needy world." Does this sound like the way your church conducts its committees, boards, and general meetings?

To begin to make these choices as mature Christians means that we will have to be "turned inside out," in Martin Luther's dramatic image. We will need to think in a new way. Since God in Christ has already secured our identity, purpose, and destiny for us, we are free from preoccupation with ourselves. We can now concentrate on others. This is real freedom—not the freedom *from* constraint only, but the freedom *to* serve with confident joy.

Moreover, to make the best possible choices, we will have to think *hard*. We will have to use and continue to improve our skills of both research and reflection to determine how best to steward the gifts and opportunities God has given us. We will have to devote our minds to regular reading, thoughtful conversation, constant prayer, and courageous decision if we are to love God and our neighbors well. We will have to think and to *keep thinking* as "growing-ups"!

Now, for all we have considered about the negative side of adolescence, we must appreciate the other side too. After all, it is all right to *be* an adolescent, and many persons emerge from that stage of life in a timely and honorable fashion! Furthermore, adolescents too often are derided by their elders. Real adolescents have a great deal to contribute to society and to societies, whether families, schools, churches, or other organizations. Their enthusiasm, creativity, simplicity, and directness would shake up many an elders' meeting, many a boardroom, many a faculty lounge—and all to the good. Leaders who really want their institutions to change for the better ought to pay more attention to adolescents. Most of the best teaching advice I have received came not from colleagues or superiors but from my students, most of whom were adolescents.

Furthermore, many adolescents are already thoughtful and loving. They do not need to be straightened out or opened up. They just need to be equipped and encouraged. They just need more knowledge and better skills. They need life experience and the wisdom that can come from it. They need more love and the opportunity to share love.

There are also churches like this: congregations that are realizing the shallowness of their theology, the superficiality of their worship, the smallness of their intellectual curiosity, and their limited perspective and resources. They do not need to be scolded and told to "settle down" and become complacent, stupefied, and "middle-aged"! They do not need condemnation. They just need help.

So for all of us, a summary exhortation. In a popular culture and a Christian subculture that promise freedom from childishness yet at times enable us to become stuck in adolescence of one kind or another, let us not become ingrown, or feel obliged to "grow out of it," or—worst of all—grow stale. Let us instead—by the grace of God—grow up.

2

The "Parachurch"

Promise and Peril

Mr. Evangelical opens the minivan door for his wife after church. Mrs. Evangelical smiles and slips into the front passenger seat. Young Evster, fourteen, climbs into the car behind his father, while Evie, nine, gets in behind her mother.

Evie clutches the various Sunday school papers she received, papers printed by the David C. Cook Company. Evster holds his student version of the New Living Translation, published by Tyndale House. Mom and Dad have placed between them in the front seat their respective leather-bound New International Version Bibles, which they bought at a discount through the Christian Book Distributors mail-order house. The family heads for home as Mom puts a new Christian music CD, the latest from Word Music, into the car stereo.

After lunch, the family prays for the Nigerian child they sponsor through Compassion International. They read the Daily Bread devotion for the day and go over the Bible verse they have selected from the Navigators' memorization program. Then they go their separate ways to relax. Evie watches a Veggie Tales video, while Evster reads the latest issue of *Campus Life* magazine. Mom works on a Christian cross-stitch pattern she bought at the local Christian bookstore, while Dad does the dishes, listening to James Dobson's program on the local Christian radio station.

It's early September, and Mom thinks about the coming week as she stitches. She practices law three days a week, and the new season of meetings of the local chapter of the Christian Legal Society starts on Monday night. Evie returns this week to her Christian dayschool, and her Pioneer Girls' club resumes at church on Tuesday evening. Evster goes to the public high school, where he is involved with the Young Life chapter. Mom herself will also make time for a neighborhood Bible study on Thursday morning.

In the kitchen, Dad is considering his own commitments. He has been asked to serve as treasurer for the local chapter of the Full Gospel Business Men's Fellowship, and yet he wants to keep helping out with the local Fellowship of Christian Athletes' ministry to the football team at his son's high school. He considers also that his mailbox has been fuller than ever with direct-mail requests for funds. And now he is getting one or two email solicitations each day. The family already contributes to a variety of organizations, including his alma mater, Moody Bible Institute, and his own favorite, Mendenhall Ministries. Pro-life groups, both in their town and nationally, receive support. He shakes his head silently. There are so many worthy causes. How does one decide what to support?

With the kitchen now clean, Dad joins his wife in the living room. "So what did you think of the sermon this morning, honey?" he asks. Their pastor, a graduate of Wheaton College and Fuller Theological Seminary, had preached a strong stewardship sermon and had included a pointed exhortation they had heard several times before.

"Make sure," he had said, "that your giving goes primarily to the local church and only after that to other good causes."

Mr. and Mrs. Evangelical settle down to try to sort it out.

Scholars increasingly contend that the kind of evangelicalism that the Evangelical family represents is best described not in terms of their church and its denomination but in terms of parachurch organizations. So says George Marsden of Notre Dame University. He describes what he calls "the evangelical denomination" as "essentially a transdenominational assemblage of independent agencies and their supporters, plus some denominationally sponsored seminaries and colleges which support such parachurch institutions." This evangelicalism, he writes, is "built around networks of parachurch agencies."[1]

1. George M. Marsden, "Introduction," in *Evangelicalism and Modern America*, ed. George M. Marsden (Grand Rapids: Eerdmans, 1984), xiv.

In their studies of American evangelicalism, Richard Quebedeaux *(The Young Evangelicals)* and Mark Ellingsen *(The Evangelical Movement)* both refer frequently to parachurch organizations as crucial to understanding the institutional shape of
evangelicalism in America.[2] Princeton sociologist Robert Wuthnow has written insightfully regarding *The Restructuring of
American Religion.* The most important change he sees in evangelicalism, as in other religious communities, is the emerging
dominance of parachurch and other "special purpose groups"
at the same time that denominational identities and organizations are eroding.[3]

The term *parachurch,* or "alongside the church," describes
those organizations that have a clear Christian identity and
purpose yet are not tied to an individual congregation or denomination. In some accounts, they do what the church in its
congregational or denominational form is not doing, is not able
to do, or is not doing well enough. This definition thus helps de-
fine a reality that Wuthnow's preferred term "special purpose
groups" does not, since Wuthnow's term includes all of the
groups within congregations and denominations—from sew-
ing circles to women's fellowships to divorce recovery workshops to international missionary societies.

Yet this term *parachurch* is seen by some as implicitly derog-
atory, and with good reason. It suggests that the "true" church
is represented only in local congregations—and whatever political structures link those local congregations together into denominations. Every other Christian organization is somehow
just "alongside" this true church: It is merely "parachurch."
Without intending this negative connotation, however, and
with full recognition that parachurch organizations as a rule
endorse the local churches and denominations in which their
own members fellowship, *parachurch* can serve usefully to
mark out this important category of Christian activity.

2. Richard Quebedeaux, *The Young Evangelicals: The Story of the Emergence
of a New Generation of Evangelicals* (San Francisco: Harper & Row, 1978);
Mark Ellingsen, *The Evangelical Movement: Growth, Impact, Controversy, Dia-
log* (Minneapolis: Augsburg, 1988).

3. Robert Wuthnow, *The Restructuring of American Religion: Society and
Faith since World War II* (Princeton, N.J.: Princeton University Press, 1988),
chap. 6.

Parachurch organizations have played an important part in the religious history of the United States and Canada for a long time. The nineteenth century saw the rise of some long-lasting and influential groups that contended for the causes of the day, whether revival, abolition, women's rights, temperance, education, or Lord's Day observance. At least as important were the domestic and foreign missionary societies that fueled what Yale historian K. S. Latourette called the "Great Century" of Christian missions. And to this day, some of the nineteenth-century organizations make a considerable mark, whether the American Bible Society, which distributes more than ten million Bibles or New Testaments annually, or the Salvation Army—itself a denomination that began as a parachurch inner-city mission.

Historian Joel Carpenter has traced the importance of parachurch organizations in the life of American fundamentalism as it went culturally underground after the debacle of the Scopes "Monkey Trial" in 1925. Through the proliferation and expansion of Bible schools and liberal arts colleges, missionary societies, evangelistic agencies, publishing houses, periodicals, and so on, fundamentalists were able to construct entire institutional alternatives to the mainline denominations and mainstream culture over which they had lost influence.[4]

But it is our own generation, in the sixty years since World War II, that has seen such groups come to rival and even surpass congregational and denominational identities and institutions for the self-definition and support of many evangelicals. Sociologists in both the United States and Canada have detailed the phenomenon of "denominational switching" and have found it most prevalent among evangelicals. Many evangelicals, that is, feel free to leave one congregation, or even an entire denominational tradition, to find what to them is most important in a church: usually some combination of the right basic doctrines, good preaching, good programs for the kids, and so on. Indeed, only among evangelicals does one encounter the revealing cliché, "church shopping."

---

4. Joel A. Carpenter, *Revive Us Again: The Reawakening of American Fundamentalism* (New York/Oxford: Oxford University Press, 1997).

What loyalties evangelicals retain more readily, however, are those to organizations of particular types that match the concerns or interests of individuals. As one can read the *Wall Street Journal* everywhere, so one can take one's subscriptions to Christian magazines everywhere. As one can often find chapters of the Lions' Club or Girl Guides in a new town, so one can find chapters of favorite Christian organizations as one moves from place to place. And as one can support a charity, political party, or alma mater from anywhere, so one can send checks to Christian charities, interest groups, and schools from anywhere.

Evangelicals certainly do support these groups. Relief and development organizations such as World Vision take in and distribute millions of dollars every year. Student ministries such as Campus Crusade for Christ staff thousands of college chapters with thousands of staff. Nondenominational seminaries such as Fuller and Trinity Evangelical Divinity School are among the largest in the world. Magazines such as *Decision* and *Christianity Today* (both arising out of the work of Billy Graham) are the most popular religious periodicals in North America. Our Mr. and Mrs. Evangelical benefit from and support a considerable number of organizations, and they select from only a small sample of the huge range of such groups.

Why so many groups, and especially since the Second World War? Wuthnow indicates that more of those groups have been founded in the last five decades than during the entire previous century.

Many groups have been formed to further traditional evangelical concerns such as missions and relief, from tiny local ministries to giants such as the Billy Graham Evangelistic Association and Feed the Hungry/Bread for the World. These ministries have been able to take advantage of the considerable increases in money and personnel available for such projects in the postwar boom.

Others have reflected a widening sense among evangelicals about what can properly be called "Christian." No more narrowness for these folks about the "Christian life" consisting merely of piety and missions! This new perspective has coincided, it seems, with the general increase in time and money for leisure activities among the population at large. Affinity groups, therefore, have been formed for Christian motorcyclists, Christian drag racers, and Christian magicians. (Indeed, some of these groups stay true to their evangelical roots as they explicitly seek to evangelize others with the same interest.) And other institutions have arisen to meet new Christian interests, such as magazines devoted to Christian contemporary music or Christian women's fashions in clothes, cosmetics, and home decor.

Still other institutions have continued the North American tradition of setting up alternatives to institutions that do not reflect or no longer reflect evangelical concerns, such as seminaries, colleges, and missionary societies. Historian Nathan Hatch's study of *The Democratization of American Christianity* points to the flourishing of this phenomenon more than a century ago, as a wide variety of new Christian groups formed in the early republic as alternatives to the inherited options.[5] This trend has only increased and spread into parachurch channels in our own day.

Periodicals such as *Christianity Today* (founded as an alternative to the liberal *Christian Century*); ecumenical organizations such as the National Association of Evangelicals (founded as an alternative to the Federal—later, National—Council of Churches); professional associations such as the Evangelical Theological Society (founded as an alternative to what would become the American Academy of Religion and Society of Biblical Literature); and even cable TV options such as CBN's Family Channel (founded as an alternative to the standard TV fare) all reflect evangelicalism's tradition of starting something else if what is available won't do.

Wuthnow's fine study points especially to the role of the state in prompting the formation of such groups. As the government has increased its involvement in spheres formerly seen as "private" and therefore at least in part under the purview of the church, so Christians have mobilized to encourage, resist, guide, or circumvent such involvement. Racial integration; free choice of abortion; the threat of taxation of clergy, churches, or other religious institutions; restraint of public displays of religious symbols; civil rights and other public recognition of homosex-

5. Nathan O. Hatch, *The Democratization of American Christianity* (New Haven: Yale University Press, 1989).

uals; the teaching of evolution in the schools—all these and more have compelled many evangelicals to act.[6]

Related to this has been the rise of new technologies and, simultaneously, a rise in confidence in those technologies to achieve worthy ends. Evangelicals who defend what many of them believe are simple, "old-time" virtues nonetheless have used the latest communication equipment and the most sophisticated organizational schemes to further their ends. Mass mailings, professional lobbyists, television and radio broadcasts, huge rallies, and even orchestrated civil disobedience are now important tools in the evangelical kit.

This growing breadth of interest, this increasing technical sophistication, and this deepening involvement in contemporary culture also reflect the higher levels of education among evangelicals, as among Canadians and Americans at large. With these higher levels of education have come exposure to and production of a multiplying of options, of both means and ends, and therefore of parachurch groups that reflect this pluralization.

One of the results of this expansion has been ironic. The founding and successes of many of these groups have prompted the formation of still other groups on other sides of an issue. The various Creation Science groups helped to inspire the development of the American Scientific Affiliation of evangelicals who, for their part, agree with some form of evolutionary theory. The rise of the New Religious Right in politics provoked responses in groups such as the Sojourners Fellowship and Evangelicals for Social Action. More recently, the formation of the Evangelical Women's Caucus and then of Christians for Biblical Equality on the egalitarian side of the gender question stirred others to establish the Council on Biblical Manhood and Womanhood in opposition.

Parachurch groups, then, clearly make up an important part—and an increasing part, it seems—of the evangelical experience.

6. I explore this theme on the Canadian side of the border in "Bearing Witness: Christian Groups Engage Canadian Politics since the 1960s," in *Rethinking Church, State, and Modernity: Canada between Europe and America*, ed. David Lyon and Marguerite Van Die (Toronto: University of Toronto Press, 2000), 113–28.

In attempting to evaluate this theme in the story of recent evangelicalism, positives and negatives go together. In the first place, much of this initiative manifests the entrepreneurial nature of North American—and especially of evangelical—Christianity. Visionary leaders and groups discern what they believe to be a need; they see that no other means will meet that need adequately; and so they plunge forward with a new solution. Great energy is added to the larger cause of Christ's kingdom, individuals' gifts are put to use, and good work is done. Indeed, some research shows that these initiatives often work synergistically rather than competitively with existing organizations (such as the local church) so that the total effort is significantly greater.

Hatch, in the tradition of historian Sidney Mead and others, has argued that this kind of organizational flexibility and adaptability is the "secret" to much of North American Christianity's "success."[7] New ventures can be undertaken without having to wait for the deliberation and consent of established authorities. Innovative programs can be instituted without having to be squared and fitted into existing structures. Gifted, enthusiastic leaders can get to work without having to receive the approval of conservative superiors. Evangelicals can get going on what evangelicals are good at: activity.[8]

The price for all this freedom, however, can be high. Without the deliberation and consent of established authorities who perhaps have a broader perspective, slight differences of approach or personal pride in leaders or supporting constituencies can diffuse resources into separate projects that are difficult (for outsiders, at least) to tell apart. Without having to complement existing structures, innovative programs can spin off into extremes and draw people away from tried and true endeavors. Without having to receive the approval of conservative superiors, individual leaders can end up reinventing wheels long

7. Hatch follows Sidney E. Mead, *The Lively Experiment: The Shaping of Christianity in America* (San Francisco: Harper & Row, 1976).

8. Evangelicals' activism is sufficiently characteristic of the movement that David Bebbington cites it as one of four descriptors of evangelicalism in his influential definition. See *Evangelicalism in Modern Britain: A History from the 1730s to the 1980s* (London: Unwin Hyman, 1989), 10–12.

since invented or, worse, unwittingly promoting harmful new enterprises.

Other strengths and weaknesses follow. There can be wonderful freedom in parachurch work for gifted leaders to get new things going and organizations to do what they believe God wants them to do. But when such leaders succeed, they can fall victim to the big shot syndrome. At the top of their own little (or sometimes quite big) pyramid, answerable to no one except their adoring constituency and handpicked board and surrounded by people who either think they are wonderful or had better act as though they do (since their jobs depend on Mr. or Ms. Number One), these big shots get into trouble. They declaim publicly on all sorts of issues beyond their competence. They make decisions unilaterally that they would never have made before without consultation with respected colleagues. And they shut themselves off from anyone who could offer them a corrective word of advice. This situation is exacerbated because evangelicals have so successfully constructed a network of alternative institutions that those institutions now are mutually reinforcing, with the same speakers, singers, and authors acclaimed all over the continent in one or another subcultural "circuit" that sometimes smells of self-satisfaction rather than the "aroma of Christ" (2 Cor. 2:15).

For their part, successful organizations can follow a related pattern. Rooted in no long-standing tradition, they initially are free to innovate here or there at the behest of their visionary leadership. But as they grow, they tend to grow bureaucracies and wear ruts of established practices. The initial flexibility and vigor can give way to a rigid and dampening "instant tradition" of "what we have always done" (that is, for the last decade or so). New ideas are perceived as threats to the established order as, in the terms of sociologist Max Weber, the original "charisma" of the group becomes "routinized." And when the first generation of pioneers moves on, and especially when the beloved founder goes to his or her reward, there can be a crisis of identity and stability: Who are we and what do we do now?

Organizations such as the Evangelical Council for Financial Accountability (ECFA) can help their members keep some of their practices respectable. But the democratic nature of such parachurch groups means that they may find support whether or not the groups behave themselves according to standards such as those of the ECFA. If the leadership can mobilize the required support and stay on the right side of the law, all sorts of things can happen—and, of course, all sorts of things have been happening all around us.

So big shots continue to drive away creative people (as "rivals" or "insubordinates") from their ministries, or they disgrace their ministries through personal scandal born of arrogance. Organizations interfere with or steal support from one another, duplicating work already done well by others but not in "our particular way." Worthy long-term projects languish for lack of support while short-term "urgent" projects—whose resource requirements are easily conveyed in punchy direct mailings or television spots—continue.

Indeed, here is just one example of how the media can tempt one to shape the message, with evangelical organizations constantly hitting the panic button to elicit support. And only recently have considerable numbers of evangelicals begun to raise questions about how much the use of such techniques—sometimes known as "the hard realities of fund-raising"—in fact threatens the integrity of those who seek to represent the truth of the gospel.[9]

Parachurch groups devoted to particular tasks and drawing on particular kinds of people can concentrate resources powerfully on important needs or difficult problems. But such groups can also foster a tunnel vision that sees the future of Christian morality, the fate of the country, or even the success of the gospel itself in terms of the success of their one particular cause. "How can you call yourself a Christian," they imply—or even declare outright—"if you do not support us in this time of trial and opportunity?" Lost is any broad sense of the body of Christ working at various complementary callings simultaneously to further the kingdom in its multiple dimensions.

Conversely, evangelicals more and more resemble people in the culture at large who, sociologists tell us, increasingly live fragmented lives, with this particular group/activity/identity for

9. For a number of reflections on these questions, see Larry Eskridge and Mark A. Noll, eds., *More Money, More Ministry: Money and Evangelicals in Recent North American History* (Grand Rapids: Eerdmans, 2000).

work; and that group/activity/identity for entertainment; and this group/activity/identity for spirituality; and so on. Rather than viewing and living life as an integrated whole, modern people tend to make up their lives as they go along, selecting from what sociologist Reginald Bibby calls "religion à la carte."[10] And as they freely select what they like, they are also free to "de-select" what they don't. Any group that disappoints them can be dropped from their list of allegiances. Here is the freedom of the consumer, and a dangerous freedom it is for both individuals and organizations.[11]

Therefore, in leaving the sturdy, if necessarily confining, identity and community of a denomination behind, some evangelicals exist in a piecemeal kind of "generic evangelicalism" and risk drifting into a scattered collection of particular allegiances to particular causes furthered by particular parachurch groups. They have no overarching framework to set things in order, to determine the relative importance of things, and to sort it all out.

Perhaps the pastor at Mr. and Mrs. Evangelical's church, then, missed the mark when he called on his congregation to give first to the local church. It is true that evangelicals in fact do give to and support a wide range of parachurch groups without necessarily giving to the local church first. But given the undeniably Christian work that so many parachurch groups do, it is not clear that his advice is based on good theology. Surely the church of Jesus Christ is present in such devoted organizations, and surely the kingdom of God extends through many of them.

Yet within that plea perhaps lies a fair warning. If evangelicals continue to place a greater proportion of their money and energy into the "free market" of parachurch organizations; if they continue to lionize superstar preachers, authors, and other celebrities whose authority is mediated by and responsible to no one other than God and their own publics; if they have little doctrinal, liturgical, or institutional identity other than the conglomeration of their own selected parachurch and church groups,

10. Reginald W. Bibby, *Fragmented Gods: The Poverty and Potential of Religion in Canada* (Toronto: Irwin, 1987), chap. 4.

11. See Rodney Clapp, ed., *The Consuming Passion: Christianity and the Consuming Culture* (Downers Grove, Ill.: InterVarsity, 1998).

will they recognize false prophets when they come, as Jesus said they will? Will they discern what is enduringly important over what is hysterically "urgent"? Will they keep their feet against the consumerist tide of our culture? Will they wisely invest in the most profitable ventures possible for the kingdom of God?

Caring, ongoing, integrating Christian communities are necessary to meet such challenges. When the challenges arise, however, who will be there to help Mr. and Mrs. Evangelical—not in Wheaton or Grand Rapids or Colorado Springs or Orlando and especially not in cyberspace but in their living room?

3

A Double Copernican Revolution

Leadership and Membership in the Church

For from him and through him and to him are all things. To him
be the glory forever. Amen.

I appeal to you therefore, brothers and sisters, by the mercies
of God, to present your bodies as a living sacrifice, holy and acceptable to God, which is your spiritual worship. Do not be conformed to this world, but be transformed by the renewing of
your minds, so that you may discern what is the will of God—
what is good and acceptable and perfect.

For by the grace given to me I say to everyone among you not
to think of yourself more highly than you ought to think, but to
think with sober judgment, each according to the measure of
faith that God has assigned. For as in one body we have many
members, and not all the members have the same function, so
we, who are many, are one body in Christ, and individually we
are members one of another. We have gifts that differ according
to the grace given to us: prophecy, in proportion to faith; ministry, in ministering; the teacher, in teaching; the exhorter, in exhortation; the giver, in generosity; the leader, in diligence; the
compassionate, in cheerfulness.

Romans 11:36–12:8 NRSV

Joshua once came running to Moses, anxious that some Israel-
ites were apparently receiving God's Spirit and so perhaps becoming rivals to Moses. Moses (whom the Bible calls the most
humble man on the face of the earth [Num. 12:3]), replied fer-
vently, "Are you jealous for my sake? I wish that all the LORD's
people were prophets and that the LORD would put his Spirit on
them!" (Num. 11:29). Wouldn't it be great, Moses says with all

the insight of a true man of God, if all God's people were full of his Spirit!

Fifteen hundred years later, Moses conversed with Jesus Christ on the mount of transfiguration. Perhaps, as he discussed Jesus' impending passion, he also looked forward a few months to the realization of Joel's prophecy—and Moses' own desire—at Pentecost:

> "In the last days, God says, I will pour out my Spirit on all people. Your sons and daughters will prophesy, your young men will see visions, your old men will dream dreams. Even on my servants, both men and women, I will pour out my Spirit in those days, and they will prophesy."

> Acts 2:17–18

This vision is worthy of a prophet, even the great prophet Moses. It is the vision of God himself for the church of Jesus Christ.

What, however, do we see in the North American church today? In particular, do we see patterns of leadership, responsibility, ministry, and affirmation that demonstrate the coming of the Spirit in the fullness of Pentecost? Do we witness the church of Jesus Christ living the way the apostle Paul said that churches should in his Epistle to the Romans?

We have instead pastors who see themselves as the center of the church, as those uniquely appointed to ministry. Therefore, the term *ministers* is applied only to them. This status shows up on church letterheads on which the names of the paid staff are printed as if they alone are the executives of the organization. We also witness this in the curious phenomenon of pastors welcoming other members of the church to a meeting, or thanking them for coming to the service, or for giving to the church, or for serving it in some capacity. All of this might make one wonder, Whose church is it, anyway? Why are *you* thanking *us*? Are you the "vicar of Christ" and speaking for him? Is this *your* church? Not to put it too bluntly, friend, but we didn't come here for you! We didn't give our time and money to you!

As we look beyond the clergy, in many congregations we see churchpeople who are quite happy to place the pastor up high on a pedestal, following the pastor mindlessly, expecting the pastor to do all the work, to take all the initiative, to make all the decisions. When the pastor finally speaks at a committee meeting or congregational gathering, such churchpeople accept his judgment as authoritative and vote accordingly.

This syndrome of status and responsibility poses several dangers. First, since the pastor is just one person, there is then only "one person's worth" of ministry that gets done—only the amount of study, evangelism, discernment, visitation, counseling, caregiving, teaching, and so on that one person can do. Multiply the staff, and the increase in ministry rises only arithmetically per person added.

Second, this set of attitudes threatens the humility of the pastor, encouraging him or her to think more highly of himself or herself than one ought to think and to attempt more than one can accomplish. Clergy burn out trying to accomplish everything they are asked to do, which is one *church's* worth of ministry, not one individual's.

Third, it reinforces the laziness of much of the rest of the church. The rest of us get to enjoy the self-centered, self-indulgent passivity of a consumer rather than take on the challenge of serving as a participant. We can "recline and receive" rather than stand, walk, and work.

Fourth, it allows insecure and conceited pastors who are threatened by the gifts of others to keep them out of influence and service. Only those with seminary education can preach. Only those with ecclesiastical titles can preside at services. Only those who have clerical credentials can offer vision and direction.

In many other congregations, however, we can witness a different syndrome. In this pathological situation, congregations view themselves as the center of the church. The pastor serves them, and he or she better do what the congregation tells him or her to do. Churchpeople have no respect for clerical expertise and gifting—indeed, in the worst cases, for *anyone's* particular expertise and gifting. They consider (in an excess of democratic leveling) everyone's opinion as important as anyone else's on all matters, even matters requiring theological, financial, administrative, psychological, or other special knowledge and experience.

Deacons or elders can be particularly guilty of this attitude. Since they exercise leadership and perform at least some pastoral functions in most churches, they can begin to think that there is no need for someone with particular clerical training and gifts. Some unusual congregations in fact might not need such help. But wise leaders have a good grasp of their strengths and weaknesses, their abilities and limitations. They stay open to the possibility that they might well have to use some of the money with which God has blessed them to support staff members to do jobs well that otherwise would be done badly, if at all.

This syndrome of "we're all the same here" poses its own dangers. First, the church fails to benefit from the gifts God has given to individuals for the good of the whole. Some people just know more than others about some things, and they should be listened to with appropriate respect—not uncritically, of course, but with the genuine concern to profit from their advice.

Second, competent resource people will eventually become discouraged if they see that their gifts are not valued. The trained pianist who sees that just about anyone who wants to do so can accompany singing, the dynamic teacher who sees that no one checks for competence before assigning Sunday school classes, or the insightful elder who looks around the room to see few colleagues who have a broad vision and administrative grasp of the church—how long can we expect such people to serve with enthusiasm? Eventually, most will leave such a congregation and seek a place where gifts are recognized and affirmed, and they can serve the Lord with freedom.

Interestingly, the two syndromes are not mutually exclusive. There can be apparently contrary dynamics in which pastors are simultaneously lionized and yet seen fundamentally as prize employees of the congregation: perhaps the way a corporation publicly champions its president, or a sports team glorifies its best player. The CEO or superstar athlete enjoys a certain amount of power that goes with the prestige of the position, but underneath the glitter it is clear who finally holds the keys, the cards, and the purse strings.

Such a combination of dynamics in a congregation naturally produces serious problems in both clerical leaders and laypeople. First, such a combination can produce a "martyr" complex in the pastor—a complex that I suspect is widespread in contemporary North American Christianity. This complex manifests itself especially when pastors get together behind closed doors to talk about their work—say, at local ministerial fellowships or pastors' conferences. "Yes, I'm terribly overworked and underappreciated," the refrain runs, usually with a heavy sigh. "But I am the servant of the Lord" (and thus especially spiritual and self-sacrificial, it is understood), "and so I will carry on." It rarely comes out as melodramatically, of course, but this attitude shows up in many ways, perhaps especially in dark pastoral humor and painful anecdotes of hellacious church board meetings.

This combination also produces a childish, consumerist complex in other churchpeople: "Pastor, you be the head—and also the hands and the feet and the legs and the arms. We'll be the stomach and also the conscience." Or, to outsiders, in confidence: "Yes, the pastor is overbearing and arrogant. You wonder, sometimes, who he thinks he is, and who's really in charge here. But he *is* the pastor, so I suppose there's not much we can do about that—unless he finally goes too far, of course, and then we'll fire him."

Let's thus take a brief look at the passage from Romans that began this chapter.

In 11:36, we clearly read that the pastor is the center of the church. . . . Well, no, we don't. We read that the *congregation* is the center of the church. . . . Wrong again. We read, in fact, that *God* is the center, and not us. What our troubled churches need, therefore, is what might be called a "double Copernican revolution" in which we finally view God—not clergy and not laity—as the center of all things, and Christ alone as the head of the church.

The opening verses of chapter 12, therefore, urge us to serve *God* according to *his* will and not according to the patterns of this world. Such proscribed patterns would include leadership patterns of lord and servant, whether the clergy are lord or servant in such a relationship. And they would also include any sort of sheer democracy in which everyone occupies the same place and role as everyone else.

Verses 3–8 carry this forward to the implication that we are Christ's body, his instrument of work in the world. Christ's body has many different parts, as we recognize that diversity is from

God, but we are one unit in Christ and therefore in each other (v. 5). As a result, we are to exercise our gifts according to our maturity, our measure of faith, and the grace given to us, and we are to do so in the best interests of one another and of Christ.

Most fundamentally, we see here—and throughout the New Testament—that in the Christian church there are to be no self-congratulating martyrs and no self-centered slackers. There are to be no super-Christians and no sub-Christians. There are just *Christians*—and yet Christians who are individual in each of their abilities and inclinations, suited for particular service within the variegated and united body of Christ.

An old joke: "There are two kinds of people in the world: those who divide the world up into two kinds of people, and those who don't." The Christian church, however, is not "two kinds of people," clergy and laity, but *one* people with different constituents: different members playing roles appropriate to their gifts and maturity. Notice, in fact, that the text describes various gifts, and those usually associated with leadership are mixed in with the rest, with no special status. To be sure, elsewhere in Paul's writings he encourages Christians to seek especially those gifts that most edify other people rather than oneself (notably 1 Corinthians 12–14). But here the very order of his list reinforces the complementary point of the mutuality and equality of gifts and members of the body.

Indeed, many Protestants and Catholics today are seriously reconsidering the idea of once-for-all ordination to pastoral ministry, finding very little basis in the New Testament for this practice of specially commending some to this peculiar role. Some, instead, have begun commending all believers to lifelong ministry. Others commend particular believers to all sorts of particular, definite ministries, as in the case of missionary journeys in the New Testament. Many Christians are coming to see various pernicious problems arising from the custom of lifetime ordination: from theological professors who abuse their clerical status for tax purposes (as they do not, in fact, shepherd any congregation), to elitism and pride on the part of some pastors who carry their sense of superiority into every situation, to a crushing burden of responsibility on the consciences of those relatively few who are ordained.

The New Testament, by our standards today, seems curiously uninterested in church political structures—to the consternation of polemicists through the ages who have championed one or another ecclesiastical polity. (Sorry, folks, but you just can't properly read congregationalism or presbyterianism or episcopalianism right out of the Bible.) The New Testament emphasizes instead two things. First, it teaches that all members are important, all members should be expected to serve, and all members should be honored as they do so. Second, it stresses that the point of the various gifts and roles is to edify the body, to extend Christ's mission of service to the world, and to bring honor to him. Thus the New Testament offers, as it so often does, a set of intensely *practical* concerns.

This instruction suggests, then, several things. First, we should reconsider the appropriateness of the common model of an individual pastor serving a local congregation. This is a role perhaps appropriate in a pioneer missionary situation in which the pastor is literally the only spiritually mature person in the church, but it is questionable in a church of many mature persons. Indeed, most church polities already include some kind of board, session, vestry, or consistory that ostensibly serves alongside the pastor in pastoral leadership. People in these roles should be expected to shepherd the church *with* "the pastor." They should not be expected or allowed to sit back and "just make decisions," much less merely rubber-stamp a domineering pastor's wishes or sit in lofty judgment upon an earnest pastor's efforts. In fact, I suggest a change in nomenclature to make this point clear for contemporary Christians. Instead of perpetuating the odd words *deacons, elders,* or *vestry members*—as useful as they have been in making certain dimensions of these roles clear—I suggest we routinely call these people *pastors,* as we expect them to shepherd the church in this overarching way.

(What about, say, a "youth pastor" or "pastor of Christian education" who is a specialist in ministry and not equipped to help shepherd the entire church? Either call him or her a "youth leader" or "director of Christian education" instead, or make it clear that "youth" or "Christian education" modifies the noun "pastor" in such a way that this person may or may not serve on the pastoral/shepherding/overseeing board, depending on his or her gifts and calling for such further responsibilities.)

Second, we should appreciate and encourage all Christians to use their gifts. Such appreciation and encouragement will have to be programmatic, of course, and not merely the theme of one or two sermons. Worship services, for example, should be varied according to the particular nature of the congregation and structured to make use of all the appropriate gifts in the church. They should not follow the common model of Christians watching a show put on by the pastor and the musicians. Church ministries should be as diverse as the congregation and the communities they serve. Church decision making should draw systematically on the wide-ranging resources of the congregation, not just on those of an elite, much less an individual pastor.

Third, we should properly value leadership. Those who truly lead with ability and an attitude of service should be valued as equals—no more important in the kingdom of God than others, but no less important either. Too many people in pastoral ministry have been discouraged by a congregational attitude of "I'd rather opt out of this commitment. Fortunately, we can always count on the pastor to do it."

Too many are burned out by a congregational attitude of "if the pastor doesn't show up at this meeting/funeral/hospital bed/ softball game, it doesn't really 'count,' and we will feel unappreciated by the church."

Too many are frustrated by deacons or elders who think they are just as good at preaching, counseling, and leading as the pastor is but who do not trouble themselves to understand the church through laborious service, who have too little formal training and practical experience, and who in fact are mere dilettantes, conceited amateurs who would wreck a church if ever given too much authority. (This is not a rant: I've seen it happen.) To be sure, part-time pastors can be just as good at this or that aspect of pastoral ministry as full-time ones. Any part-timers who want a place at the pastoral table, however, had better count the cost and deserve to be there on the basis of ability, attitude, and activity.

Too many are stressed out by a congregational attitude of "whatever you say, we will do—unless you push us too far or demand too much, in which case we won't discuss it but will simply replace you." A lack of good dialogue, of clear communication of concerns and apprehensions, prevents leaders from understanding and therefore offering appropriate guidance for their congregations until—*snap!*—it's too late, and the pastor faces an angry dismissal.

Those who lead—pastors, other church staff, committee chairs, and so on—ought to be people of real ability and godliness. And if they are, then we ought to trust and respect them. They ought to be people whom we should, in fact, *follow*. But we follow as "workers together," walking, as it were, side by side. As they provide leadership, we provide our resources to the common cause and indeed contribute to their leading, whether by advice, encouragement, or labor.

Graphically, we can consider a metaphor different from the cosmological, "Copernican" one. Instead of a triangle with the pastor and other leaders at the top and the rest subservient and passive below, and instead of an inverted triangle at the pointed base of which an exploited leader suffers the weight of too many demands from too many people, we should rotate the triangle in the air to become horizontal. Yes, leaders are at one point, since all lines in the church have to reach them for them to perform their roles properly. But they are no higher or lower in status than anyone else. They are just doing their jobs, as everyone else does his or her own, and the rest of us then spread out to take each of our proper places in the wide work of the church.

If the church wants to thrive, it must do what Christ, the head of the church, tells it to do. There is too much to accomplish—as there was in Moses' time, in Peter's time, in Paul's time, and in our own time—for us to sit back and expect God to do it all through a special class of clergy. There is also too much work to do, however, for us not to take full advantage of the gifts Christ has given to each local congregation.

If every congregation heeded this passage and related New Testament teachings with full seriousness and resolve, if every congregation determined to share the responsibility of ministry throughout its members, if every congregation honored all those who serve in all the ways they serve, if every Christian was full of the Spirit and active in ministry, the church of Jesus Christ would advance. The gates of hell itself would not prevail against it.

4

Evangelicals and the Bible

Yesterday, Today, and Tomorrow

The B-I-B-L-E
Yes, that's the book for me!
I stand alone on the Word of God
The B-I-B-L-E!

All Christians love and venerate the Bible, but no tradition of Christianity loves and venerates it more than evangelical Protestantism. The renowned English pastor and writer John R. W. Stott, one of the current generation's leading evangelical statesmen, pronounces evangelicals to be, above all, "Bible people."[1] Lutheran sociologist Peter Berger famously writes of Protestants purging Roman Catholicism of most of its myth and mystery, leaving the Bible at the core of humanity's revelational connection with God.[2] Evangelicals "stand alone on the Word of God" as faithfully as any Protestant—even to what many Protestants, including most Lutherans, would deem an extreme. Precisely because of this setting aside of other religious resources in favor of the Bible, the identity, activity, and vitality of evangelicals have depended crucially on the Bible in their midst.

This chapter offers three sketches of the role of the Bible among evangelicals, especially evangelicals in "cultural" North America (that is, Canada and the United States). The first is the historical sketch: how the Bible has figured in evangelical life over the last couple of centuries and especially in immediately

1. John R. W. Stott, *Evangelical Truth: A Personal Plea for Unity, Integrity, and Faithfulness* (Downers Grove, Ill.: InterVarsity, 1999), 65.
2. Peter Berger, *The Sacred Canopy: Elements of a Sociological Theory of Religion* (Garden City, N.Y.: Doubleday), 110–13.

preceding generations. The second is sociological and journalistic: how the role of the Bible is under stress amid sweeping changes in contemporary evangelicalism. And the third is prophetic—or, more modestly, merely "punditic": how individuals and organizations who care about the Bible can encourage evangelicals to continue to love and venerate it in the new century before us.

My thesis, then, is simple and threefold. The Bible has played an enormous and complex role in evangelical life. Almost every feature of that role, however, is under challenge today. Those challenges are not likely to disappear, and therefore, evangelicals and others who share their regard for the Bible will need to meet those challenges with pious hope and prudent discernment.

Who Are the Evangelicals?

An academic cottage industry has sprung up in the last generation of historians, sociologists, and theologians to answer the question, Who are the evangelicals? Since the answer is only preliminary to our purposes, let's agree on a widely accepted general definition.[3]

Historically, evangelicalism emerged in the eighteenth-century revivals associated with the work of John and Charles Wesley, George Whitefield, and Jonathan Edwards. Individuals and movements who descend from these origins and have not departed from the concerns that marked them can be called "evangelicals," along with those groups that latterly identified with these concerns and the network of groups that espouse them. Evangelicals thus would be found among Methodists, Presbyterians, and Baptists in the former set and among, say, the Mennonite Brethren and the Christian Reformed in the latter.

Evangelical concerns are perhaps best seen as a cluster of five. First, *evangelical* comes from *evangel,* or "gospel." Evangelicals

---

3. Cf. David W. Bebbington, *Evangelicalism in Modern Britain: A History from the 1730s to the 1980s* (London: Unwin Hyman, 1989), 1–19; George M. Marsden, "Introduction," in *Evangelicalism and Modern America,* ed. George M. Marsden (Grand Rapids: Eerdmans, 1984), vii–xix; and John G. Stackhouse, Jr., *Canadian Evangelicalism in the Twentieth Century: An Introduction to Its Character* (Toronto: University of Toronto Press, 1993), 6–12.

prize the classic good news of God being in Christ, reconciling the world to himself. Doctrinally, then, evangelicals are creedally orthodox (whether or not they happen to recognize the authority of the Apostles', Nicene, and Chalcedonian Creeds, which many do not) and concentrate particularly on the career of Jesus Christ—his incarnation, life, death, resurrection, and ascension. Evangelicals believe that only in the work of Christ is salvation secured and only through faith in Christ is salvation normally received.[4]

Second, evangelicals hold to these beliefs and their other religious tenets because they believe the Bible teaches them, and the Bible is the Word of God in written form. "Jesus loves me—this I know, for the Bible tells me so." The Bible is fully inspired by God such that it is God's own book; it does not contain merely God's signature, as it were.[5] Most evangelicals specify that the Holy Spirit inspired the very words of Hebrew, Aramaic, and Greek in the Bible's canonical form, while others believe that God allowed the limitations of the human authors to show up in relatively minor matters. All agree, however, that the Bible is the fundamental and supremely authoritative reference for religious life, once given by God in inspiration and subsequently taught by God's Spirit in the illumination of all who read it in faith.

Third, evangelicals believe in conversion, and they believe in it in two respects. Each person, because of each person's inherited sinfulness and many individual acts of willful sin, must be converted away from sin and toward God, raised from spiritual death to eternal life—in a phrase, "born again." Furthermore, evangelicals believe in "full conversion"—a life of increasing holiness, of disciplined and fervent piety that more and more conforms to the pattern of obedience and goodness set by Christ himself until one reaches complete maturity, or "glory," in heaven.

Fourth, evangelicals believe in mission. They particularly support the work of evangelism, the act of proclaiming the gos-

---

4. I am leaving open the issues of disagreement between evangelical "restrictivists" and "inclusivists." I try to clarify this nomenclature in "An Agenda for an Evangelical Theology of Religions," in *No Other Gods before Me? Evangelicals and the Challenge of World Religions,* ed. John G. Stackhouse, Jr. (Grand Rapids: Baker, 2001), 189–201.

5. So Nicholas Wolterstorff, *Divine Discourse: Philosophical Reflections on the Claim That God Speaks* (Cambridge: Cambridge University Press, 1995).

pel and calling for a decision regarding it. But they also cooperate with what they see to be the divine mission in the world, especially the amelioration of evil. Thus, they have sponsored hospitals, schools, farms, and other institutions that care for the body and the mind as well as the spirit.

So far, of course, these four emphases are generically Protestant and, with the exception of the emphasis placed on the supremacy of scriptural authority, basically Christian. What makes evangelicalism distinctive is its fifth emphasis, namely, its transdenominationalism. Evangelicals hold the other four concerns so primary that they recognize as kin anyone who holds them and are willing to work with others on that basis. Thus, evangelical Pentecostals, Methodists, Anglicans, and Mennonites, for example, all share the first four concerns and go on to cooperate in the World Evangelical Fellowship, World Vision, InterVarsity Christian Fellowship, and a multitude of other institutions. Those Christians who happen to affirm the first four concerns but do not privilege them or see them as a sufficient basis for fellowship and service (for example, some Mennonite, Baptist, and Lutheran groups) would thus not be called "evangelicals" in this context, however truly gospel-oriented and thus "evangelical" they are in a more basic sense.[6]

Evangelicals and the Bible: The Past

Christ and Salvation

The "original evangelicals" were, of course, the sixteenth-century Protestant Reformers who saw themselves as champions of the true gospel against Roman Catholic distortions and accretions. The famous Reformation slogans—*sola fide, sola gratia,* and *sola scriptura*—epitomized the Protestant agenda of stripping away the husk of medieval superstition that had obscured the gospel kernel for centuries.

Modern evangelicals have continued to understand Christ and salvation in terms that self-consciously reject Roman Catholicism's putative excesses: all those intermediary saints and clergy;

6. Donald W. Dayton and Robert K. Johnston, eds., *The Variety of American Evangelicalism* (Downers Grove, Ill.: InterVarsity, 1991).

all those rituals, pilgrimages, and relics; all those extra duties entailed by confession and penance; all those elaborations of the cosmos such as limbo, purgatory, and various angelic realms; and all those dubious additional doctrines, whether the immaculate conception of Mary or the infallibility of the pope.

Indeed, it is this last doctrine that highlights the role the Bible plays in the evangelical articulation of the gospel, for evangelical self-understanding is that evangelicalism teaches what the Bible teaches—nothing more and nothing less. Roman Catholics, however, teach much more, drawing as they do on what they understand to be divinely inspired tradition mediated to the church through the centuries and clarified particularly in the *magisterium,* or "teaching office," of the church personified by the pope. Evangelicals are radically Protestant in this respect: The Bible is a sword that evangelicals use to cut through Roman Catholic teaching and practice that is not conformed—to evangelical satisfaction, at least—to the teaching of Scripture alone.

Evangelicals see a symmetry here. Roman Catholics teach "too much," adding unhelpfully to the gospel message, in large part because they draw on "too much" in the way of revelational resources. Disqualifying tradition as inspired revelation and ignoring Catholic claims of papal authority, evangelicals are reduced to sorting out what the Bible says. This reduces the version of the gospel they preach to a simpler, even starker, message.

The other tradition over against which evangelicals have defined themselves since the origin of evangelicalism in the eighteenth century is liberal theology. To be sure, most textbooks trace the origin of liberal theology to the career of F. D. E. Schleiermacher, whose first book was not published until 1799.[7] Yet some of the polemics of Jonathan Edwards—perhaps most famously his treatise *On the Freedom of the Will* (1754)—address theological positions that clearly anticipate nineteenth-century liberalism.[8]

Whereas evangelicals believe Roman Catholics add improperly to the "store" of God-given revelation and thus end up with

---

7. Friedrich Schleiermacher, *On Religion: Speeches to Its Cultured Despisers,* trans. John Oman (1799; reprint, New York: Harper Torchbooks, 1958).

8. Jonathan Edwards, *Freedom of the Will,* ed. Paul Ramsey (1754; reprint, New Haven: Yale University Press, 1957).

a theology and piety that are too elaborate, evangelicals believe liberals subtract from the Bible's authority and thus commend a theology that is attenuated in every major respect. According to evangelicals, in liberal theology, the incarnate Son of God shrinks down into a "very, very, very, very good man," in the acidic phrase of H. Richard Niebuhr. Salvation becomes merely our imitation of Jesus' example of godliness—without need of atonement. In many versions of liberalism, the Christian religion itself becomes just one of many salvific paths to God. Evangelicals also oppose liberal theology's "irreverent" and "destructive" historical criticism of the Bible and its preference for contemporary reason and experience over the orthodox doctrine harvested faithfully from the pages of Scripture over the centuries. They believe, therefore, that liberalism is left with a thin theology and a merely moralistic (and perhaps mystical) piety wrought out of a thoroughly corroded Bible.

Positively, then, evangelical summaries of doctrine typically provide proof-texts for each proposition, not only as glosses but as authorities: We believe X because the Bible teaches it *right here*. Orthodoxy is *not* merely the position of the strongest party in church disputes. Evangelicals maintain instead that orthodoxy is simply a digest of the Bible in correct delineation and emphasis.

The Bible

The evangelical commitment to *sola scriptura* has played out in a number of respects, some of them paradoxical, some of them even contradictory. Evangelical theology was formed in the crucible of the Enlightenment, and much of it continues to show traits of that movement. Evangelical sermons and Bible study materials, for example, typically emphasize "word studies," the tracing of etymologies and semantics through the Bible. Evangelical laypeople often possess reference volumes of this sort (*Vine's Expository Dictionary* being perhaps the most popular)[9] in their home libraries. Such word studies often depend on Enlightenment-style univocity, that "one word means

9. William E. Vine, *Vine's Expository Dictionary of Old and New Testament Words* (Nashville: Nelson, 1997).

one thing." Thus, many evangelicals confidently discuss a term such as *glory* or *righteousness,* flipping lightly over vast tracts of scriptural material with the aid of their concordances. Here, ironically, is a built-in disregard for hermeneutical context, a disregard that punishes the blithe exegete all the more when symbols are in play: Thus, "fire" *always* connotes "judgment," and "leaven" *always* connotes "sin."

The most obvious sign of evangelical regard for the text of Scripture is the habit of proof-texting. Evangelicals assume that truth is found in the very words of Scripture, and therefore, they can demonstrate that every truth (at least every truth of faith and religious practice) emerges from particular texts of the Bible, cited by chapter and verse. Such an inclination is not confined to the more radical "biblicistic" evangelical traditions either—whether Plymouth Brethren, Mennonite, or Baptist. Luther and Calvin, Edwards and Wesley, Hodge and Finney, Moody and Graham—evangelical theologians, scholarly or popular, habitually cite actual verses of Scripture as the authority for whatever point they wish to make.

Many evangelicals, however, have been slow to take stock of just what role should be played, and in fact is played, by reason, experience, and tradition in their theologies. John Wesley formulated his famous "quadrilateral" to coordinate these four resources, but few evangelicals outside the academy have explicated what goes on in their theology besides mere Bible study. Thus, the dispensationalist congratulates herself that her system is merely the end result of careful exegesis, not a paradigm that, once adopted, bends recalcitrant texts to its pattern. The Calvinist does the same, ingenuously claiming that his system is merely the distillation of biblical truth.

The most obvious giveaway of such a lack of theological self-consciousness is the widely recommended evangelical practice of inductive Bible study. Taught in dispensational Bible schools, denominational seminaries, and transdenominational Bible study guides alike, the practice of inductive Bible study seeks to expose the Bible reader to the text without the interference of "theology" or "tradition." Readers instead are given a particular passage to read (but who selects the beginning and end of a passage and according to what criteria, when the earliest manuscripts of the Bible have neither paragraph or sentence divisions?) and customarily are provided with a few "guiding questions" meant to help the reader come to his or her own conclusions (albeit within the terms of the questions interposed between the reader and the text!). The Reformation doctrine of the "perspecuity of Scripture," therefore, plays out in evangelical regard for and reading of the Bible in ways that are sometimes perplexing and even self-defeating.

The authority of the Bible as evangelicalism's primary theological resource is reinforced in evangelical use of the scriptural text symbolically. Scripture texts are calligraphed or cross-stitched for decorating rooms both domestic and ecclesiastical. Bible texts in some evangelical traditions replace even the cross as the symbol emblazoned on the front wall of the sanctuary— in an aesthetic that resembles Islam's resistance to pictorial representation and embrace of the Quranic text for both ornamentation and devotional focus.

What is true of the biblical text is true also of the Bible itself as a holy object. A massive Bible typically adorns a prominent lectern at the front of the church—in some traditions, occupying the place of honor reserved in other churches for the elements of communion. In traditional evangelical homes, one can count on each family member owning a leather-bound, gilt-edged Bible. One can also count on these Bibles being shelved in places of honor, with many evangelicals practicing the folkway that no other book shall be placed on top of a Bible. Each family member possesses a personal Bible because evangelicals typically mark important rites of passage with the presentation of a new Bible: birth and (perhaps) infant baptism, beginning a new phase of education, believer's baptism or confirmation, graduation from school, and marriage. Such Bibles often include pages for the recording of milestones in one's life, just as the family Bible serves as the register for the life of the clan. In these and other ways, then, evangelicals affirm the preeminence of the Bible both practically and symbolically.[10]

10. Colleen McDannell, *Material Christianity: Religion and Popular Culture in America* (New Haven: Yale University Press, 1995), 67–102.

Conversion

Conversion in the sense of evangelism will be discussed under "Mission" below. Conversion in the sense of the progressive transformation of the sinner into the image of Christ is an equally important theme in evangelicalism.

When evangelicals get together to worship, the Bible always figures prominently. Evangelicals have long championed preaching as the focus of the worship service. Good preachers are valued everywhere but in no tradition more than in evangelicalism—so much so that the pastor is sometimes referred to simply as "the preacher." The sermon normally comes at the climax of the liturgy, and evangelical sermons are almost always longer than they are in non-evangelical churches.

Evangelical sermons tend to feature the actual words of Scripture. Many preachers simply exposit the Bible book by book, chapter by chapter, verse by verse. Others follow a lectionary or set of themes, but the evangelical impulse is always to refer frequently to the text of the day. "Let's look now at verse X" is a familiar phrase in evangelical churches, with the expectation that people will have their Bibles open throughout the sermon to follow along to see that the Bible does, in fact, say what the preacher says it does. Evangelical churches typically have pew Bibles, but regular attenders bring their own Bibles and, commonly, take notes on the sermon either in the margins of those Bibles or in pads brought along expressly for that purpose. People in evangelical churches typically expect to learn more about the Bible each time they hear a sermon.

Scriptural knowledge is to be gained in other ways as well. Children in evangelical Sunday schools hear Bible stories, not just cute fictions meant to illustrate Christian truths. They learn the order of the books of the Bible and engage in contests (known colloquially as "sword drills," from Eph. 6:17 and Heb. 4:12) to find a particular passage first. They are also encouraged to memorize Scripture, whether key verses or entire passages such as the Ten Commandments or the Beatitudes.

Adults also typically engage in Bible study in a small group, whether a class on a Sunday morning or a midweek home fellowship. Laypeople commonly own at least one single-volume commentary on the Bible and often invest considerable sums in a reference library of biblical commentaries, concordances, and other study aids. Such aids assist them in their personal study and devotional reading that, again, normally focuses on Scripture (as opposed to, say, devotional readings from the church fathers or contemporary spiritual writers).

Scripture is also embedded in music. Adults sing Scripture in church, from sixteenth-century psalters to Vineyard Church's compositions, while Sunday schools feature Scripture songs for the kids. Indeed, many evangelical children learn most of the "memory verses" they know by singing them rather than merely reading them.

The role of Scripture in forming Christians, whether individually or in community, also emerges in verbal clues offered by the by. Ethical issues are discussed in church boardrooms, at annual meetings, and in Christian homes with reference to snatches of Scripture: perhaps a proverb here or a beatitude there. Allusions and catchphrases show up as a matter of course in informal speech at church dinners and in correspondence with other believers. And jokes are made, whether from the pulpit or over Sunday lunch, that presume a knowledge of the Bible that is sometimes very specific and might include in particular a knowledge of the King James Version (e.g., "Who was the first smoker in the Bible? Rebekah, because she lighted off a camel [Camel]"; "What man had no parents in the Bible? Joshua, the son of Nun [none]").

The Bible is woven throughout the evangelical subculture. It naturally plays a large role, then, in the witness of this tradition to the larger world.

Mission

Evangelicals have a long record of providing for the needs of others at home and around the world. But when evangelicals offer help—medicine, education, food, or other things—they typically tie it to evangelism.

Furthermore, evangelicals do not merely commend the gospel to others. They argue for its validity and virtue, and they do so typically with open Bibles. Therefore, the apologetic as well as the evangelistic modes of evangelical mission deserve a look, and both show once again just how important the Bible is to evangelicalism.

In apologetics, evangelicals typically concentrate attention on the Bible because it is, again, the supreme guide to their faith. Thus, evangelicals argue for the historical reliability of the Bible's accounts, the prophetic accuracy of its predictions, the beauty of its poetry and prose, the glory of its moral teachings, and the fundamental reality of its divine inspiration and authority. On the basis, then, of this peerless volume, others are invited to look at the Bible's central subject, Jesus Christ, and come to faith in him.

In the act of articulating the gospel message, evangelicals do not rely on only the Bible's authority for the truth of that message. They use the Bible in that proclamation quite directly. Heeding promises such as "my word . . . shall not return unto me void" (Isa. 55:11 KJV), evangelicals freely salt their presentations with phrases, verses, and even chapters of Scripture. Billy Graham epitomizes the evangelical who confidently proclaims, "The Bible says . . ." even to audiences who are not yet convinced of the Bible's authority. Graham *is* convinced, and so he speaks and reads from it with assurance that the very words of the Bible are charged with divine blessing and will be used for the divine mission by the Holy Spirit in the evangelistic encounter. Evangelicals at Bible schools and evangelism training workshops offered in their local churches or by groups such as the Billy Graham Evangelistic Association are taught to memorize key Scripture texts at the heart of the gospel and urged to deploy them in evangelistic conversations. The Bible is not seen as magical, as a book of charms merely to be recited to effect the desired outcome. But it is trusted as the vehicle through which God promises to work as a matter of course.

Thus, evangelicals not only learn the Bible themselves to aid them in witnessing to the gospel but also encourage their neighbors to read it in the course of their investigation of the Christian faith. Such reading means that evangelicals have worked hard to make Scripture available to their neighbors—which brings us to our last heading.

Transdenominationalism

In order to venerate the Bible, to use the Bible, to learn, memorize, teach, and evangelize from the Bible, the Bible has to be intelligible and available. Thus, evangelicals have enthusiastically supported means of translating and disseminating the Bible. Whether individuals struggling to produce translations on missionary frontiers—with the pioneer missionary William Carey and his Bengali translation as the epitome of such efforts—or major international organizations, with the Wycliffe Bible Translators/Summer Institute of Linguistics perhaps the best known, evangelicals have worked hard and even sacrificially to render the Bible in the various languages of the world.

Evangelicals have worked no less diligently at the tasks of producing and transporting Bibles. Colporteurs in the last century brought Bibles to the borderlands of rural and urban America alike, to remote farmers and forgotten slum dwellers. In our time, Brother Andrew, "God's smuggler," has inspired a generation of evangelicals with his swashbuckling escapades on behalf of Scripture distribution behind the Iron Curtain.[11]

In these tasks, evangelicals typically have worked cooperatively with other evangelicals, for nothing is more basic, more uniting, and less contentious among evangelicals than the value of the Bible. The great Bible societies, therefore, arose as mainstays of evangelical ecumenism. Translation projects became one of the few enterprises in which evangelical scholars of various traditions worked together—in our day producing the New American Standard Bible (1960), the New International Version (1973), and the Living Bible (notably its revised edition, 1997), among numerous versions issued among Anglophone North Americans.

The culture of North American evangelicalism, then, features the Bible in every important respect. And in every important respect, the place of the Bible is under challenge in North American evangelicalism today.

Evangelicals and the Bible: The Present

While the traditions of evangelical regard for and use of the Bible continue to the present, in each area of concern new challenges have arisen.

11. Brother Andrew et al., *God's Smuggler* (New York: New American Library, 1987).

Christ and Salvation

In academic theology among evangelicals, three areas of debate have opened up in this generation, each of which has the Bible at its heart. The first two fit nicely under this first heading regarding the gospel message. The third deals with the nature and function of the Bible itself.

The first question, then, is the question of world religions and the fate of the unevangelized. All evangelicals reject the option of "pluralism," the position associated with scholars such as Wilfred Cantwell Smith and John Hick and with varieties of Hindu and New Age religion, which affirms all spiritual paths as salvific—or, at least, affirms all *good* spiritual paths as salvific. (No one wants to endorse, say, infant sacrifice before Moloch in the ancient world or National Socialism in our own era.) But evangelicals divide into two broad camps of "exclusivists" and "inclusivists" on the question of the salvation of those who do not hear and understand the propositions of the Christian gospel.[12]

Exclusivists maintain that hearing and responding to the gospel is normally required for salvation (hardliners would remove the qualifier "normally") and that the best one can hope for others is that God might do some mysteriously gracious thing about which we have no clue. Exclusivists, of course, have their proof-texts, such as Romans 10:14 ("How shall they hear without a preacher?" [KJV]) and Acts 4:12 ("For there is no other name under heaven given among mortals by which we may be saved" [NRSV]).

Inclusivists respond that the Bible is full of examples of people who have saving faith without knowledge of Jesus Christ: Most obviously, every believer in the Old Testament qualifies as such. Furthermore, inclusivists press, what about infants, the mentally incompetent, the schizophrenic, or others who are incapacitated and cannot understand the propositions of the gospel? Surely God will not abandon them all?

12. John Sanders, *No Other Name: An Investigation into the Destiny of the Unevangelized* (Grand Rapids: Eerdmans, 1992); and John Sanders, ed., *What about Those Who Have Never Heard? Three Views on the Destiny of the Unevangelized* (Downers Grove, Ill.: InterVarsity, 1995).

Both sides, to be sure, deploy both proof-texts and examples. Exclusivists point to Cornelius as an example of a God-fearer to whom, nonetheless, God sent Peter to bring him the gospel (Acts 10); inclusivists wield verses such as John 10:16: "I have other sheep that do not belong to this fold" (NRSV).

This debate has yet to mature into a full-blown theology of religions, although there are some new ventures in that direction.[13] Neither side, however, is challenging fundamental orthodoxies regarding Christ or salvation, and both clearly see the Bible as the fundamental resource for exploring and resolving this conflict.

The same terms apply to a controversy much more far-reaching than the inclusivism-exclusivism debate. Led by theologians Clark Pinnock and Gregory Boyd, some evangelicals have reacted strongly against what they see to be a view of God distorted by Platonism via the Augustinian tradition.[14] This view of God, they believe, portrays him as static in his timelessness, loveless in his impassibility, and utterly domineering in his sovereignty. This new group recommends that evangelicals prize the "openness" of God: God goes through time as we do, feels in some way as we do (whether love or hate, dismay or celebration) as events come and go and as his purposes are frustrated or fulfilled, and cooperates with his creation toward an ultimately beneficent end.

The majority of evangelical theologians currently look askance at this movement. Some agree with its unhappiness with the classical categories of timelessness, impassibility, and so on but believe that many streams of evangelical orthodoxy provide the resources to differ with those categories without adopting what seem dangerously close to the categories of process thought, albeit without the Whiteheadian vocabulary and detail. Others denounce the enterprise as simply heretical, compromising the

13. Clark H. Pinnock, *A Wideness in God's Mercy: The Finality of Jesus Christ in a World of Religions* (Grand Rapids: Zondervan, 1992); and Gerald R. McDermott, *Can Evangelicals Learn from World Religions?* (Downers Grove, Ill.: InterVarsity, 2000).

14. Clark H. Pinnock, ed., *The Openness of God: A Biblical Challenge to the Traditional Understanding of God* (Downers Grove, Ill.: InterVarsity, 1994); and Gregory A. Boyd, *God of the Possible: A Biblical Introduction to the Open View of God* (Grand Rapids: Baker, 2000).

glory of God both metaphysically and morally: God is no longer omniscient and omnipotent and is himself subject to doubt, confusion, and fits of rage from which he needs sometimes to be talked down (e.g., Exod. 32:7–14).

It is stories such as these in the Bible, of course, that provide grist for the "openness" mill, and openness theologians have developed their theology considerably beyond these perennial Bible puzzles. The openness advocates fundamentally assert, then, that they are simply reading the Bible better than their opponents—indeed, that they are more faithful to the text of the Bible and less dominated by non-Christian philosophical presuppositions.

No one in this debate doubts the creedal affirmations regarding Christ and salvation as far as they go. Clearly, however, the nature of God's work in Christ, the nature of God's program of salvation, the nature of the church's relationship with God, and the eschatological hope of the church are all affected by the change in viewpoint advocated by the openness model.

The Bible

The third leading edge of evangelical theological development rises entirely to the level of methodology. Whether in the championing of Karl Barth's theology by an earlier generation of evangelical theologians, most notably Bernard Ramm and then Donald Bloesch, or in the exploration of postliberal views in the current one, evangelical theologians have been wondering aloud about just what biblical inspiration and authority mean.[15] Some have come to the conclusion that the Barthian/postliberal acceptance of higher criticism followed by a kind of "second naïveté" that affirms the Bible's truth and authority within the discourse of the Christian community point the way out of two hundred years of controversy between evangelicals and liberals. Many evangelicals, however, wonder whether the Barthian/postliberal program does anything other than sidestep the question that both traditional evangelicals and liberals want to keep asking: However "true" the Bible seems to be for those within the Christian fold, what claims can be made, if any, for the truth of the Bible in the world at large?

15. Gary Dorrien, *The Remaking of Evangelical Theology* (Louisville: Westminster John Knox, 1998).

Is the Bible just "our book," in some importantly limiting way, or is it really God's book to the world?[16]

Such methodological debates have yet to seep very far into evangelical popular culture. What is striking in some cutting-edge evangelical churches is a sort of embarrassment toward or at least a downplaying of the Bible as symbol. Seeker-sensitive churches typically avoid traditional religious symbolism, and this includes the Bible, in their buildings. No great Bible sits splendidly at the front of these auditoriums. Rarely are Bibles available for those in the pew to read. Instead, if viewing a biblical text is deemed necessary, it is projected on to a screen or wall for a few moments and then, surely with unintentional irony, extinguished. Or perhaps a few verses are printed in the program for that service, to be discarded as so much trash once the service is finished. Now, cheap shots are easy to score against such churches by those who neither understand nor sympathize with their agenda. But it remains a matter of fact that the Bible is purposely much less evident in these meetings than in traditional evangelical sanctuaries.

As for the Bible in the private lives of evangelicals, some still have Scripture texts on the walls of their homes, but this practice is fading fast. As for other kinds of adornment, evangelicals do not typically go to the Hasidic extreme of binding actual texts to their bodies, of course—but some now wear T-shirts emblazoned with snatches of Scripture, use ballpoint pens and pencils imprinted with more, and even buy candy and gum that "bear witness" via Bible verses on their wrappers. The "Jesus junk" of contemporary evangelical paraphernalia contrasts sharply with former evangelical traditions of the Bible as a holy object.

Conversion

Evangelical preaching in many places is as traditionally expositional as ever, but two other traditions of preaching are increasingly vying with it. Evangelicals influenced by the "narrative" school of homiletics (American Fred Craddock is perhaps the best known in this tradition) are encouraged to reach the

16. Timothy R. Phillips and Dennis L. Okholm, eds., *The Nature of Confession: Evangelicals and Postliberals in Conversation* (Downers Grove, Ill.: InterVarsity, 1996).

postmodern mind by jettisoning the old, linear, argumentative form of preaching and adopting an impressionistic, quick-cutting style that emphasizes storytelling over declamation.

In the Pentecostal and charismatic wings of evangelicalism, preachers still unabashedly wave open Bibles as they speak and still quote Scripture aplenty. The Bible, that is, continues to occupy the sermon both symbolically and materially. But many of these preachers perpetuate a "ranting" tradition of homiletics that ironically also fits into some people's understanding of the postmodern mind: its preference for the episodic, allusive, and affective. In this style of preaching, the speaker selects a theme and then proceeds to make his points in turn while studding each one with portions of Scripture—sometimes an extended quotation, often merely a quick phrase. The effect is not unlike the more refined homiletics of the narrative school in the combination of storytelling (or "testimonies"), scriptural allusions, and punchy exhortations.

What is difficult to judge in either form of quickly changing kaleidoscopic presentations is whether what the preacher is saying really emerges from the authoritative Word of God, or whether the preacher might just be grabbing convenient bits from here and there to justify a point he was going to make anyway. Such sermons increasingly resemble MTV videos as nonsequential, rapid-fire "experiences," and it becomes unclear whether anyone is learning much about the Bible.

Evangelicals apparently are still learning about the Bible in small group studies. Yet many of these groups read other sorts of books together, whether guides to a healthier marriage or family life, handbooks on evangelism or apologetics, or even popular Christian novels. To be sure, any and all of these pursuits can be part of a good program of adult Christian education, but an observer might still wonder where, if not in these groups, evangelicals are engaged in an ongoing study of the Bible.

Preachers report, and pollsters on both sides of the border confirm, that churchgoers and non-churchgoers alike show a declining grasp of even basic Bible content.[17] The experiential-

---

17. Reginald W. Bibby, *Fragmented Gods: The Poverty and Potential of Religion in Canada* (Toronto: Irwin, 1987); and George Gallup, Jr., and Sarah Jones, *100 Questions and Answers: Religion in America* (Princeton, N.J.: Princeton Religion Research Center, 1989).

cum-therapeutic cultural wave of the late twentieth century has tended to turn even genuine Bible studies into encounter groups in which people offer their impressions of "what this Bible passage means to me" or perhaps, in good evangelical pragmatist fashion, "what this Scripture encourages me to do," without lingering on the prior question of "what the Bible actually says." "Sword drills" are quaint relics of a rapidly disappearing subculture, as is the discipline of Scripture memorization. Indeed (to take the phenomenon of humor seriously as an anthropological marker), one could not tell a joke to a typical church audience today that assumed a particular item of scriptural knowledge with confidence that everyone would get it.

The Bible, in short, is disappearing on several fronts within evangelical precincts, as well as in the culture at large.

Mission

In terms of apologetics and evangelism, traditional methods and resources still prevail. Evidentialist and rationalist apologetics dominate the market, and most evangelistic programs still emphasize proof-texts as part of an appropriate gospel presentation.

The rise of "friendship evangelism," however, is not without its ambiguities. At its best, such an emphasis encourages evangelicals to eschew the bad old days of seeing neighbors as souls to be saved, as targets for proselytization. The gospel is lived out and in time is articulated within the context of genuine love for one's neighbor. At its worst, however, such an approach allows for the benign and inoffensive vagueness of mere goodwill without the specificity and challenge of a scripturally informed conversation.

At the other end of the scale lies the popular Alpha program, originating from Holy Trinity-Brompton (HTB) Anglican Church in London, England, and readily imported to North America in recent years. In many respects drawing on previous evangelistic programs, most notably the supper meetings of the Oxford Group Movement of two generations ago, the Alpha program has been employed enthusiastically by groups that share neither HTB's Anglicanism nor its charismatic emphasis.

And therein lies the rub, for this presentation of "basic Christianity" is actually devoted largely to a clearly charismatic presentation of the work of the Holy Spirit in the individual and the church, from the controversial teaching of the baptism of the Holy Spirit in classical Pentecostal terms to extended discussion of spiritual gifts. Such teachings, however true they might be to the charismatic tradition in its distinctive cultivation of believers, seem oddly prominent in a program designed to evangelize those who do not attend church and are not confessing Christians of any sort. Indeed, they seem oddly out of keeping with the evangelistic emphases of the New Testament itself, which concentrates instead on the saving work of Jesus Christ, particularly in its accounts of apostolic proclamation.

One wonders in both cases, then, how deeply informed by the Bible evangelical thinking has become nowadays even in regard to the fundamental enterprise of Christian mission.

Transdenominationalism

When it comes to the projects of translating and disseminating the Bible as key zones of evangelical transdenominational cooperation, one might conclude that the evangelical story is an entirely happy one. Domestic translations have proliferated with huge sales across denominational lines. Publishers have devised more and more ingenious "niche" Bibles to serve what they perceive to be the needs of homemakers, fathers, mothers, professionals, youth of various ages, college students, divorced persons, pastors, evangelists, apologists, and other groups. And international translation continues apace, with Wycliffe Bible Translators weathering various storms, from accusations of complicity with the CIA overseas to the kidnapping and even murder of some of its staff.

Yet all has not been well even here. Controversy over English translations—not a new phenomenon, of course—most recently rocked American evangelicalism concerning the proposed revision of the New International Version (NIV). The NIV, evangelicalism's most popular modern translation, was revised as it had been previously for a new edition. This time, however, inclusive language for human beings in various places was systematically included. (The New Revised Standard Version [1989] had anticipated this change by a decade.) Some prominent evangelical scholars and activists took umbrage at what they saw to be the not-so-thin edge of a feminist wedge that would lead, perhaps, to outright goddess worship as inclusive language spread like a virus throughout the Bible. Many evangelicals saw these fears as hysterical, but the American publisher backed off and refused to print the new edition. (The British publisher had already begun distribution.) Actual matters of Bible translation are indeed at stake in good faith: There might well be something important lost, for example, in rendering Psalm 1 as "Blessed are those" (that is, a group) rather than the more literal "Blessed is the man . . ." (that is, a faithful individual). But more than a few observers have seen the conservative reaction as beholden at least as much to anti-feminist ideology as to scriptural fidelity. In that respect, this was the first translation controversy *not* clearly about ortho-dox doctrine of God, Christ, and salvation but perhaps about secondary or even tertiary matters of differing evangelical opinion.[18]

Other critics believe the very proliferation of translations has affected evangelical piety and community. No longer are the cadences of a single translation (the King James Version, or KJV) familiar to everyone and therefore useful for reference and allusion. Evangelical congregations are now filled with people who have to translate between the version they brought to church and the version from which the preacher is reading. Furthermore, the new translations have aimed so obviously, and generally successfully, at offering contemporary idiomatic and accessible English that many critics bemoan the loss of nuance and poetic singularity of expression that made the KJV a classic of English literature. "Who wants to memorize this banality?" some ask.

Finally, the phenomenon of the "niche" Bible, usually published with a variety of Bible "helps," prompts some to wonder whether evangelicals are unwittingly reintroducing a whole new set of intermediaries between the reader and the text. Moreover, these intermediaries are not nearly as distinguished as, say, Thomas Aquinas, Augustine, or other saints, but are merely contemporary Bible scholars, popular pastors, or simply hack writers hired to find material somehow germane to the target group.

18. John G. Stackhouse, Jr., "The Battle for the Inclusive Bible," *Christianity Today* 43 (1999): 83–84.

Furthermore, the very attempt to package these Bibles in various covers and designs to appeal to this or that taste has had the unfortunate symbolic effect of conforming the Bible to an individual's chosen "lifestyle" rather than marking it out as a holy object to which one ought to conform one's lifestyle.

In all of these respects, and doubtless more, the changes in evangelicalism have involved important changes in the way evangelicals regard and use the Bible. What, then, lies before those concerned to assist evangelicals in these respects on the road ahead?

Evangelicals and the Bible: The Future

To remark that evangelicalism has changed is to spout a truism. Every movement changes over time, and evangelicalism has taken on the contours of a succession of cultural impulses from its eighteenth-century origins to its current position at the beginning of a new century and millennium. So, too, have evangelicalism's relationship to and use of the Bible varied over time and in several subcultural versions. The mere fact, then, that the present does not look like the past should not necessarily provoke either dismay or joy.[19]

Change, indeed, often brings both loss and gain and sometimes both unavoidably together. The case of the Bible is a splendid case in point. This last section traces some of these combinations and concludes with suggestions as to how foreseeable changes can be negotiated most helpfully by those who promote the Bible among evangelicals.

Christ and Salvation

Doctrinal controversy can distract the church from its worship, fellowship, and mission when only trivial matters are at stake. But discussion of the fate of the unevangelized or the

19. Bebbington, *Evangelicalism in Modern Britain;* Nathan O. Hatch and Mark A. Noll, eds., *The Bible in America: Essays in Cultural History* (New York: Oxford University Press, 1982); and Mark A. Noll, *Between Faith and Criticism: Evangelicals, Scholarship, and the Bible in America* (San Francisco: Harper & Row, 1986).

nature of God in the openness controversy are hardly trivial matters.

As the religious pluralization of North America proceeds apace, the task of understanding other religions in theological terms becomes more and more urgent—not merely establishing grounds for apologetic polemics but also clarifying just how these religions figure in the providential plan of God. The authority of the Bible is a key touchstone for such discussions, both in its inspired portrayal of God's revelation to Israel and the church in the context of other religions and also in the very question of the authority of the Bible vis-à-vis other sacred scriptures. Thus, the popular controversy nowadays regarding the canon of the New Testament that excludes the Gnostic gospels ultimately leads to the question of the *world's* "canon" and the place of the Bible among the Qur'an, Bhagavad Gita, Dao De Jing, and so on. Suddenly, it seems, theologians and pastors need to dust off their class notes regarding the emergence of the biblical canon and consider afresh just why this set of ancient books was judged to constitute God's holy Word in a way that no other books were. Those who seek to promote regard for the Bible can aid the church by reminding us of those principles of canonization in the midst of a plethora of alternatives.

As for the question of the openness of God, this is hardly a matter of mere metaphysical speculation, as all sides agree. Pastors always struggle to explain God's providence to those who are earnestly trying to make life decisions, improve their prayers, or deal with suffering. The openness dispute touches on all of these matters and more. One pastor involved in this discussion reported that this was the first time in his twenty-year career that his churchpeople were fascinated by a theological subject. In their fascination, he continued, they were reading and discussing the Bible as never before concerning matters that, he concluded with satisfaction, really matter.

The Bible

The methodological conversation between evangelicals and postliberals remains mostly within the academic cloister, but it has immediate ramifications for every evangelical's use of the Bible: How does one profit best from higher critical commentary? How do we apply the Bible to our lives or to the church's life today? What role can the Bible play, if any, in conversations with neighbors who do not grant its divine authority?

As for the role of the Bible in public worship, missiological as well as liturgical sensitivity will continue to be the key to striking the right balance for any Christian group seeking to honor God in its particular setting among its particular neighbors. Keeping Christian symbols to a minimum in a seeker-sensitive meeting can be easily defended on the grounds of hospitality, the way one might be careful not to overwhelm guests in one's home with Christian symbolism upon their first visit. But hospitality also requires "truth in packaging," that we present ourselves honestly at first and always. Critics of the seeker-sensitive model have yet to be convinced that such wholesale evacuation of Christian symbols from the meeting place does not in fact amount to a fundamental misrepresentation of the Christian ethos at the actual heart of the meeting. The best of these churches, however, make clear that such meetings are not aimed at Christians but at seekers. Thus, when the church gathers for its own worship and fellowship (so this logic proceeds), Scripture is given its proper symbolic prominence, congregants are expected to bring their own Bibles, and the teaching is as expositionally substantial as in any other church.

The use of biblical texts to adorn various paraphernalia is also not a new issue. Scriptural texts and motifs bloomed throughout many nineteenth-century American and Canadian homes, whether on walls or on teapots. Critics must be careful, therefore, to ensure that their criticism is not just a matter of aesthetic taste dressed up in theological robes. What to one person may be a sacrilegiously tacky bathroom mirror Scripture text or T-shirt slogan might be another person's daily reminder to piety or a heartfelt testimony to salvation. Some uses of the Bible, yes, might well be the result of misplaced zeal or crass commercialism and deserve denunciation as such. These phenomena, however, challenge everyone concerned with the dignity of the Bible to recall just what the Bible was given to us to do and to beware of an excessive reverence that would prevent the Bible from functioning as fully as it should in people's lives.

Conversion

Few would suggest that North America enjoys a golden age of preaching at the turn of the new millennium. Preaching that blithely strays from the solid path of the biblical text leads no one to a good end over time. Blame, however, cannot be laid solely at the door of this or that homiletical style. Most pastors are so busy with the multitude of tasks with which most churches encumber them that *any* sort of sermon in *any* style that shows *any* serious preparation can be commended. If churches want pastors to preach the Bible well, they must equip pastors with the time, space, and books to do it.

Adult Christian education, with a strong component of Bible teaching and a continual theme of relating all of learning to the Bible, should constitute an essential part of evangelical church life. It does, indeed, in many congregations, but hardly in most. A sermon or two per week, expositing a few verses or perhaps a chapter or two, is hardly a sufficient diet of scriptural teaching. Furthermore, the very genre of preaching rarely lends itself to the discussion of matters that should show up in a class, whether historical questions of the provenance and purpose of a particular Bible book, the geographical situation, its context in the canon, and so on. In small churches, pastors might be assisted by only a few laity, if any, with the expertise necessary to teach these subjects well. Such churches must again decide whether they will assist the pastor in other works of ministry in order to free him or her to prepare and deliver this teaching.

What is true for adult Christian education goes for youth programs as well. Entertainment and socialization into quiet behavior too often seem to be the priorities of Sunday school teaching, with a little moralizing to take home. Evangelicals have done better than most other religious believers in North America in retaining the allegiance of their youth into adulthood. But the sad state of most churchgoers' knowledge of the Bible testifies to the poor quality of Sunday school teaching such "cradle Christians" have received. Evangelicals of previous generations took such teaching seriously, holding regular seminars and rallies for Sunday school teachers and encouraging young people to go to Bible school to equip themselves for lifelong ministry as lay volunteers in such programs. Such a note of concern for the quality of Christian education is heard rarely today outside larger churches that can afford to hire Christian education specialists.

One bright note must be acknowledged, however, regarding the knowledge of Scripture among children. Cassette tapes and CDs with Scripture songs have lulled many a child to sleep at night, and an increasing number of Bible stories have come to life on video. Evangelicals have been quick to use these new media to bring the Bible to children, and it is through them that many children are learning what they do know of its text and narrative.

Evangelicals used to be accused of being "biblicistic" and even "bibliolatrous" as they reflexively referred any problem of life to a Bible text. That accusation can rarely be leveled anymore, and it is not necessarily because evangelicals have become more theologically sophisticated. Many instead have become just as ignorant of the Bible as anyone else.

Mission

Some evangelical apologists and evangelists have left behind the inherited models and have adopted a different posture and voice in their public addresses. Such defenders and commenders of the faith now offer the Christian tradition without claims to its universally demonstrable superiority. Instead, they acknowledge respectfully the outlooks of others and offer the Christian tradition to such others with the acknowledgment that Christians do not have a corner on truth and goodness but do believe they have been introduced to the God who is Truth and Goodness. Such apologetics and evangelism do not give up traditional confidence in the Christian tradition, but they do take seriously the postmodernist *and Christian* teaching that humans are both finite and fallen, and therefore, each must humbly offer what he or she has found to his or her neighbor without pretensions to absolute certainty.[20]

Thus, the Bible is offered without embarrassment as "our book" for the consideration of one's neighbor in the same way

20. For example, Thomas V. Morris, *Making Sense of It All: Pascal and the Meaning of Life* (Grand Rapids: Eerdmans, 1992); and John G. Stackhouse, Jr., *Can God Be Trusted? Faith and the Challenge of Evil* (New York/Oxford: Oxford University Press, 1998).

he or she might loan an evangelical a copy of the Adi Granth or the Book of Mormon. Those who seek to equip evangelicals for such exchanges, therefore, might well consider publishing Bibles with front matter that introduces it to those who do not have a Christian background.

As for passing trends in evangelistic technique, they will come and go, and time will sift them. But while they are among us, evangelicals who know the Bible will be responsible to serve the church by doing some sifting as well. In the best cases, such people will reshape these evangelistic approaches to resemble more closely both the examples and teachings of the Bible. In the worst cases, such people must point out the incompatibility of such approaches with biblical norms.

Transdenominationalism

The controversy over the inclusive-language NIV raises two important questions for evangelicals: the issue of gender in both society and the Bible (over which evangelicals continue to argue), and the perennial translation tension between striving for intelligibility to a particular culture, on the one hand, and remaining faithful to the foreign cultures of the Bible's own literature, on the other. While some critics in this controversy appear to be straining over linguistic gnats or chasing paranoid fantasies, others have raised valid points that cut to the heart of how the church tries to understand God's Word and make that Word understandable to its neighbors. Those who promote the Bible, therefore, have the opportunity to equip the church for truly edifying argument by teaching the church the principles of good Bible translation and warning about the inevitable differences of opinion that result even among people of goodwill and sound skills. Such a teaching opportunity can not only promote regard for the Bible but even more importantly remind Christians of the command to love one another even in, and especially in, the midst of passionate dispute.

The production of Bibles with various "helps" interposed between the reader and the text is hardly a new phenomenon for evangelicals. Many today continue to accept C. I. Scofield's famous notes as simply a digest of scriptural truth, bound as they have been for almost a century with the King James Version. Those who promote Bible reading today need not retreat into a "Bible alone" purism, since everyone who reads necessarily brings along some sort of interpretative framework. But the fair-minded critic might yet wonder about the propriety of giving just one celebrity pastor's view of things in a version bearing his name when evangelical transdenominationalism could bring a number of orthodox viewpoints to bear on scriptural commentary and reduce the risk that mere idiosyncrasy will substitute for community wisdom.

One might also pause before agreeing with the criticism of modern translations that they are so banal as to be unfit for memorization, particularly when compared with the putative majesty of the King James Version. As revisers of the KJV itself have agreed through the centuries, there is little to be gained spiritually by memorizing words that in fact have changed in meaning over time, let alone become simply opaque. Furthermore, the Bible itself is not uniformly written in fine style. There is, therefore, a fundamental translation question here not to be overlooked: If Peter or John wrote like fishermen, shouldn't their epistles sound that way, rather than sounding like the prose of a highborn wordsmith—or sounding more or less the same as Paul, Matthew, Isaiah, and Solomon?

An old question of Bible use also resurfaces in the age of the Internet, CD-ROMs, and hypertext. Electronically stored and accessible Bibles have been a great boon to preachers, scholars, and students of the Bible. Yet the specter of Thomas Jefferson methodically cutting and pasting the Bible into a form that met his own ideological preferences looms over hypertext versions of the Bible. Does the convenience of these electronic editions militate against the sense of fixed authority that printed Bibles convey? Will Scripture readings be presented to churches nicely pruned of objectionable phrases or stories?

One must be careful not to overreact in this regard. Lectionaries already routinely tell readers what parts of which psalms are appropriate for public reading and which parts (even to the division of a verse) should be left out. New technology does not necessarily entail either blessing or bane: As Neil Postman tirelessly reminds us, new media bring new ways of doing things, with gain and loss necessarily combined.[21]

21. Neil Postman, *Amusing Ourselves to Death: Public Discourse in the Age of Show Business* (New York: Penguin, 1985).

At the dawn of a new century, it would be well not to attempt too much prediction. Historians can assure a public eager for prophecy of the future that whatever they predict will, in many respects, be either wrong or incomplete. What those who love the Bible do not doubt, however, is that "the word of our God stands forever" (Isa. 40:8) and will accomplish God's purposes in the next century—whether via paper, phosphors, or media as yet not invented—just as it has in the previous twenty.

5

A Complicated Matter

Money and Theology in North American Evangelicalism

The contrasting economies of heaven and earth collide in Frank Capra's well-known film *It's a Wonderful Life*. The hero, George Bailey, has fallen victim to the financial stupidity of a dotty uncle and faces ruin and disgrace. Considering suicide, he is rescued by an earnest angel, Clarence Oddbody. As Clarence tries to convince George that he is George's guardian angel and has been sent to help him, George offers a retort that focuses on what he perceives to be his central need: "You don't happen to have any money on you, do you?"

Clarence replies that he doesn't have any because money isn't used in heaven.

George looks up at this startling announcement and then deadpans, "Well, it sure comes in mighty handy down here, bub."

Undaunted, Clarence proceeds to help George see that what really matters in his life is not his lack of wealth but his enormous success in helping others live happy, useful lives. George eventually comes to appreciate that he has had a wonderful life after all.

The movie ends, however, with the economies of heaven and earth coinciding. George, after all, still faces jail if he cannot come up with a large amount of cash. He is rescued by all of the friends he has made through his own sacrifice, diligence, and compassion. They come through for him in his hour of need with an outpouring of donations. As George beams at the kindness of his community, a bell rings to signal that Clarence the angel indeed has done his job.

There is, to put it mildly, a wide range of views of money within the evangelical tradition in North America, as there is in the Christian church worldwide. Money is a powerful symbol. Indeed, it bears many and diverse meanings that connect with basic priorities in the lives of individuals and communities. Our own culture testifies to this fact in its strong colloquialisms: Money is equated with both the staff of life (thus she has lots of "dough" or plenty of "bread") and with odious waste (thus he is "filthy" or "stinking" rich).

Such a potent symbol, not surprisingly, shows up often in the recorded discourse of Jesus Christ. Interpreters of North American religion who have no direct access to their subjects' inner lives do well to pay heed to the ancient gospel wisdom of analyzing where the "treasure" is to decide where the "hearts" are also. Let us follow, therefore, the way money moves through the life of a typical evangelical donor and a typical evangelical institution.

Such a narrative will illumine a large and complex network of theological issues as the economies of heaven and earth overlap in the lives of Christians who are obligated by Jesus' teaching to render to Caesar what is Caesar's and to God what is God's. Recognition of the varying ways in which North American evangelicals have viewed these theological themes (highlighted in bold type) will go a long way in explaining why evangelicals have treated money in such different ways. And recognizing just how *many* theological themes—both doctrinal and ethical—are in play when it comes to money helps to explain why evangelical views and practices regarding money may at times be inconsistent: Coordinating all of these topics into a coherent theology of money is a daunting task.

Ms. Evangelical, then, goes to **work.** Does she view her work in theological terms, and if so, what terms? Some Christians have endured work as a necessary evil to be eliminated eventually in a paradise of continual ease or, as in the aspirations of mystics, ceaseless contemplation of God. Others have seen work as intrinsically good, as God himself is a "worker," and thus it is to be undertaken as part of representing the *imago Dei.* Still others have commended work as something Christians do for the time being to keep a fallen world more or less in functional order so as to preserve the raw material out of which God is fashioning the church.[1]

In each case, there is the question of locating work within a broader sense of **vocation,** of a "calling" by God to do this or that for some divinely approved reason. Does Ms. Evangelical view her work in terms of a kind of hierarchy, and if so, what values inform it? Some evangelical hierarchies, for example, have placed a premium on evangelism and thus have lionized missionaries who proclaim the gospel at great personal cost. This sort of hierarchy deprecates businesspeople who are occupied with making and spending money. Other evangelical hierarchies, however, have completely reversed the order, seeing God as the guarantor of health and wealth to all who have sufficient faith. Thus, the wealthy are the blessed, and the poor are properly suffering for their unbelief. Evangelical intellectuals, not surprisingly, have been tempted to value those whose jobs focus on ideas and "high culture." And as activistic as evangelicals typically have been, they all tend to glorify the workaholic: "Better to burn out than to rust out," as one modern evangelical hero (Jim Elliot) affirmed. Finally, does Ms. Evangelical view her work as an organic part of her broader calling as a Christian, as a component to be prudently integrated with the rest of her life's relationships (as daughter, neighbor, friend, and church member)? Or does she see herself primarily as "a physician" or "an engineer" or "a salesperson" or "a police officer"?

The situation is more complicated when a Christian understanding of vocation is perverted by less noble motives. The Reformation doctrine of the goodness of all divinely acceptable vocations, for instance, has gone to seed in some episodes of North American evangelicalism in which it has been used to justify what is at root simply hedonism. The tension, let alone the conflict, between God and Mammon thus has been resolved by seeing the two as partners. God, you see, wants me to succeed in my profession/business/career in obedience to his call-

1. This last suggestion is perhaps the most uncommon: For a recent articulation of it, see Robert W. Jenson, "The Church's Responsibility for the World," in *The Two Cities of God: The Church's Responsibility for the Earthly City,* ed. Carl E. Braaten and Robert W. Jenson (Grand Rapids: Eerdmans, 1997), 1–10.

ing and for his greater glory—so I can eat my cake and have it too, gaining both earthly goodies and heavenly glory.

So far, these themes perhaps seem to have little to do with money directly. But in this economy, as in most (but not all: Slaves, for instance, work without recompense), there are **earnings** to be expected. Ms. Evangelical's view of earnings may well depend on her view of work. What is the relationship in her mind between her labor and her wages? Are her earnings simply what "her own hand hath gotten her" according to the current market price—thus, her earnings are her own by right? Perhaps her earnings are the gracious provision of God for her maintenance and stewardship and are (strictly speaking) only accidentally related to the work she does—that is, they merely happen to be what the market pays for her work just now and are not in any sense an objective indicator of the importance of her work nor of her success in it. Ms. Evangelical might take a different view yet and see the amount of her earnings as directly correlated with her obedience to God, as blessings to God's favorites (as in the biblical phrase "he who honors me, I will honor"). Are such blessings primarily for her to spend on her own enjoyment, then, and only secondarily to help others?

Part of Ms. Evangelical's view of the matter will have to do with her view of **economics,** however articulate or inchoate. Does she see her earnings as her "just deserts" rendered by a market guided by an "invisible hand" of divine providence? Does she see her earnings instead as her not-quite-just deserts, that is, as what she deserves *at least* from a not so infallibly guided market that seems to pay those people over there too much compared to what she thinks her own work is worth? Some have said that North American evangelicals have generally tended to treat economic systems as if they were part of the climate or topography: realities simply to be dealt with as given, not as human constructs thus amenable to human revision. Does Ms. Evangelical ever wonder whether the economic system includes some basic inequities, to compensate for which she should use her money, political influence, and other resources?

How, then, does Ms. Evangelical spend her money? How does she arrive at her financial priorities? This involves the question of **ethical and theological method.** In an integrated

Christian worldview, her management of money will emerge out of her sense of God's call on her life. But where is she to learn about her vocation and particularly about a Christian view of money? Perhaps she depends most on the teachings of her pastor or of popular authors she has read—whether Christian or secular. Surely she is influenced by advertisements, both secular and Christian, but they may do little to clarify her vocation, perhaps distracting her from it instead by manipulating her through feelings of guilt or greed. To what extent is her ideal standard of living informed by the lifestyles of her favorite characters on television or in the movies? Her view of money likely depends to a great extent on the values she learned in the family she grew up in and the churches she has attended. Has she ever processed these models according to her mature Christian commitments? Does she believe her responsibility as a Christian steward requires her to conduct research into the best value for her money, whether through reading *Consumer Reports*, engaging in comparative shopping, or reading Christian newsmagazine accounts of the integrity and efficiency of this or that charity? In sum, the question of ethical method involves how Ms. Evangelical comes to her financial decisions and with whom she deems it valuable to consult.

Let's suppose she now decides to give some of her money to explicitly Christian institutions. How does she decide how much to give and to whom? In particular, she faces the category of **tithing.** Some Christian communities simply use the Old Testament figure of 10 percent of income. In our age of income taxes and many other compulsory contributions to the public good, however, is that now 10 percent of net income or of gross income? Canadians generally are taxed more than Americans to provide a more extensive social welfare program. Should that affect one's tithe? We have here the complicated question of ethical method in regard to the application of the Old Testament law of Israel to the New Testament Christian community. This is especially the case given that the New Testament contains no direct teaching regarding tithing per se.

Is the tithe owed to the local congregation for its maintenance and ministry? Is it owed, in part, to the denominational family of which the congregation is a part? Or somehow to the church universal? What about Christ's body as it is active outside the congregational/denominational structures, in so-called (and, in some ecclesiologies, badly called) parachurch organizations? Some pastors teach that InterVarsity Christian Fellowship, World Vision, Evangelicals for Social Action, or Promise Keepers deserve financial support, but only *after* the congregation/denomination gets its tithe. But is this the best way to understand the nature of the **church,** as if congregations are primary and other Christian institutions are somehow secondary?

Ms. Evangelical has made up her mind and now wants to pay. She might write a check, hand over cash, or authorize withdrawals from her bank account on a regular basis. All of these media, of course, link her with the **world** of commerce, the state ("Whose inscription does it bear?"), and society at large. Thus, a theology of money is related to a theology of **culture.** What is the world, what is culture, what are they for, and how ought the individual Christian and the Christian church relate to them in greatest faithfulness to Christ? Is Ms. Evangelical responsible, for instance, for how her bank invests the money she keeps there?

Common evangelical wisdom holds that she should tithe every pay period as her first financial obligation and then manage her money from there. Should Ms. Evangelical borrow money, therefore, whether through a loan or (more likely) through a credit card, to pay her church or some other Christian organization as well as her bills?[2] Some evangelicals have taught that indebtedness is a mark of excessive entanglement with the world, even a sort of voluntary servitude to the world, and is to be avoided at all costs. Is it right for her, then, to take on even a student loan or a mortgage, quite apart from the question of making good on her tithe commitments?

As she takes the bills from her wallet or flips open her checkbook, she confronts **money** itself. Some Christians have viewed money as a value-neutral tool, a form of power to be used well

---

2. The question of indebtedness and bankruptcy has come before the American courts of late in regard to a couple who were already in debt and in the process of going bankrupt. They gave money to a church along the way, and creditors sought to get the offerings back to pay the couple's debts. See Randy Frame, "Bankruptcy Tithes Exemption Sought," *Christianity Today* 41 (8 December 1997): 76.

or badly but itself neither good nor evil. Others have warned that it is instead a "power" as the New Testament describes such things (Rom. 8:38; Eph. 6:12; Col. 1:16) and is to be reckoned with carefully as such. Is it in fact an alternate god, Mammon, that competes with the true God for the soul's allegiance? Money is a highly complicated and multivalent symbol, performing a wide range of psychological and sociological functions for various kinds of people. How is Ms. Evangelical to view it?

The money is now dispensed. What does Ms. Evangelical think will be the **return** for her use of money in this way? Has God promised, as health-and-wealth teaching says he has, to reward her with a literally significant financial return? Will the organization she supports in this way send her a tangible premium of some sort? Does she believe instead that her "mansion" in heaven will be better furnished because of this "investment" in charity here below (Matt. 6:19–33 and par.)? Is she simply to enjoy the temporary but welcome relief of the guilt feelings that plague her from time to time, and what is she to make of this motivation as a Christian? And then there is the question of a tax receipt—which raises the interesting question of whether she needs to make sure to give *that* away too in order to make sure her tithe of 10 percent is *fully* donated.

Once the money has reached its destination, how will it be used? What is the ratio of overhead costs to ministry expenditures, and how is the organization itself to set its priorities? Each organization has to decide how much, if anything, it should put into endowment for future use and a measure of security, how much into promotion and development, and how much into immediate use, perhaps trusting God to supply day by day. Should new projects be undertaken before capital is at hand in faith that God will cover later costs? Or should they be deferred for fear of leaving the "house" half built, as the parable puts it (Luke 14:28–30)?

How is money to be raised? Executives of such organizations wrestle with how often and how hard to press the panic button to rouse their constituencies, particularly through direct-mail campaigns. Others face the question of the morality of their advertising as it resorts to sentimentality, end-of-the-world alarmism, or even criticism of competing min-istries in order to focus donors' attention on the needs of their organization.

Many missionary societies have required prospective mis-sionaries to engage in "deputation," the practice of raising one's own support from friends, relatives, and churches. While this policy keeps missionaries in touch with their supporters (for all sorts of reasons), its successful practice obviously re-quires a set of skills in some ways different from those required of, say, a Bible translator or an AIDS counselor. Critics have seen this policy to place an inappropriate burden on such workers and, indeed, to privilege successful fund-raisers over those who might be better suited for the actual work of the agency.

Each organization has to work out the connection between those who donate the money and those who decide how it ought to be spent. To what extent, for instance, do major donors dictate the spending of the organization? As North American churches have moved from legal establishment to denominations and then to a populist free-for-all, within congregations themselves there can be acute pressure on clergy to kowtow to those members whose financial support seems crucial. (This pressure is all the more obvious in other institutions lacking the biblical aura of the congregation itself. If such organizations are not doing what the people want, the people will move their money else-where.)[3] Furthermore, beneath this dynamic in churches is the very relation of pastor to people. To what extent does the perspective of the marketplace shape this relation, so that the pastor is viewed as nothing other than an employee of the church?

The other side to this question is the issue of the role of the leading personalities within the organization—especially if there is a single figure who symbolizes the organization to its public. To what extent do such individuals in fact set priorities by their power to raise funds—regardless of their wisdom and expertise concerning the actual work to be done? To what ex-

3. For the historical roots of this question, see Nathan O. Hatch, *The De-mocratization of American Christianity* (New Haven: Yale University Press, 1989).

tent is the organization shaped by the economic dependence of every employee on the charisma of the leader?[4]

The question of fund-raising interlocks with the question of image, of the way the organization presents itself. Perhaps it makes well-heeled donors feel at ease by entertaining them with fine dining and meeting them in tastefully appointed headquarters (that require expensive upkeep as part of basic operational costs). Perhaps money is spent lavishly on appearances to signify to lower-income donors that God's blessing rests upon it. Does the organization pay for high-quality print and audiovisual promotional materials in order to present its case most vividly and, to be frank, to make it stand out from its counterparts? Does the organization instead convey its commitment to thrift by economizing everywhere it can?

These dovetailed questions of fund-raising, priorities, and image remind us of a long-standing tension in Christian relations with the rich. As the church receives donations—whether from medieval lords, Renaissance magnates, early modern burghers, or Gilded Age robber barons—it seems to be offering approval. Protestants have been scandalized in this regard, particularly over the Roman Catholic practice of granting indulgences, but Protestants, too, have often been glad to offer certain laurels to donors possessed of questionable motives. (The Orthodox, whose story does not figure largely in North American history, have their own complicated heritage of relations with the powerful.) Ms. Evangelical, then, might well expect another "return" to motivate her donation: a lovely ceremony lauding her as a fine Christian patron and her name suitably inscribed on this or that monument for later generations to admire.

4. Harold John Ockenga, champion of the "neo-evangelical" movement of the 1940s and following decades, made clear his views of leadership and money in an interview he gave in his seventy-seventh year: "The pastor should sit on the board of trustees, not as a member, but just as he should sit on the board of deacons, or elders. He ought to know where everything goes. He has to raise the money, therefore he ought to be able to see where it goes. . . . He ought to have a good bit to say about the final disposition of funds. I didn't do that directly; I did it through the boards. I sat on every board that spent a dime, because I didn't want the money to go to the wrong place. It was too hard to raise" ("Harold John Ockenga: Chairman of the Board," *Christianity Today* 25 [6 November 1981]: 28).

Beyond the question of relating to the rich is the question of the economy in general—and thus we encounter again the theology of **culture.** To what extent does the church implicitly or explicitly endorse the economy in which it finds itself and particular players within it? The most crucial example of this question in American history, of course, is the defense of the slave trade. In the century and a half since then, however, Christians have continued to engage in other economic controversies, whether the rise of the free market domestically and internationally; the threat of communism; the emergence of the welfare state, especially since the New Deal and expanded through the Great Society; the furor over Reaganomics; and so on. It is easy, with hindsight, to scorn nineteenth-century evangelicals for exploiting Scripture to justify the slave-based economy of the South. Such exploitation, however, can hardly be presumed to have vanished since.

Again, we return to most North American Christians, and perhaps evangelicals in particular, treating the economy as they have the weather: complaining about it but generally taking it for granted. (This attitude might well be more true of white evangelicals than of black or Latino believers, of course, given the violent history of the latter groups' encounter with American economic forces.)[5] Evangelical holdings in church buildings, schools, missionary societies, advocacy organizations, and other institutions, however, amount to hundreds of millions of dollars, quite apart from evangelicals' own domestic and business properties, investments, and so on. Clearly, evangelicals have had a significant financial presence in America. Yet one has to look northward to Canada, to the politics of Social Credit and to the Cooperative Commonwealth Federation (now the New Democratic Party), to find broad-ranging movements, let alone political parties, devoted to economic reform with Christians at their core.

5. See Clifford A. Jones, Sr., "How a Christian African-American Reflects on Stewardship in a Consumer-Oriented Society," in *The Consuming Passion: Christianity and the Consumer Culture,* ed. Rodney Clapp (Downers Grove, Ill.: InterVarsity, 1998), 151–66; and Calvin O. Pressley and Walter V. Collier, "Financing Historic Black Churches," in *Financing American Religion,* ed. Mark Chaves and Sharon L. Miller (Walnut Creek, Calif./London: AltaMira, 1999), 21–28.

However the money comes in to an organization, then, how should its employees be paid and otherwise benefited? Some Christian organizations have paid everyone the same, while most have employed differentiating criteria, whether seniority, qualifications, experience, need, function, and so on.[6] What constitutes an appropriate standard of payment in this institution—what parallels with other institutions, if any, will be sought to peg remuneration in this one?[7] Clerical salaries have long been used by historians as measures of a church's self-image vis-à-vis the broader culture, whether farmer-preacher Baptists or highly educated and professional Episcopalian priests. Every other institution faces similar questions. Will a Christian college, for instance, compare its scale with other Christian colleges in its region, in the country, or in North America? Will it compare itself with secular schools? Will a missionary society compare itself financially with a secular charity or with a government agency? With the organization of labor in modern times comes the question of the legitimacy of unions—even in Christian "ministries." How ought Christians, whether labor or management, workers or owners, to consider collective bargaining? Some see unions as disruptive of organizational harmony and therefore to be avoided in Christian ventures. Others see them as necessary tools for promoting justice

6. Speaking of the zone I know best, namely, Christian higher education in Canada, I note that at least three approaches to faculty remuneration have been formulated that break with typical North American patterns. Prairie Bible Institute in Alberta for most of its history paid all staff members similarly, regardless of function, allowing only for marital status and dependent children. Ontario Theological Seminary in Toronto (now Tyndale Theological Seminary) had no ranks among its faculty members (everyone was a "professor" of his or her field) and paid everyone the same. And Regent College, Vancouver, did employ the typical North American ranks of assistant, associate, and full professor but paid one salary per rank, regardless of years already spent in that rank (that is, there were no "steps" in the pay scale). For more on the ethos of these institutions, see my *Canadian Evangelicalism in the Twentieth Century: An Introduction to Its Character* (Toronto: University of Toronto Press, 1993).

7. One is reminded of Billy Graham's long-standing policy of having his board pay him a fixed salary—regardless of income received by the Billy Graham Evangelistic Association—that was pegged to the typical salary of the pastor of a large, urban, American congregation (see William Martin, *A Prophet with Honor: The Billy Graham Story* [New York: William Morrow, 1991], 139).

and restraining evil. Answering these questions, then, will depend on consideration of the interlocking theological themes of **providence, vocation, mission, stewardship, community, and more.**

Christians with a well-developed doctrine of **sin** will exercise an appropriate hermeneutic of suspicion in regard to theological justifications of financial policies. Such Christians might inquire, for instance, whether the practice of paying everyone the same low salary truly exemplifies Christian community or is instead a rationalization for poor fund-raising and woolly minded administration. They might, to pick a different example, ask whether the structuring of an organization in parallel with secular bureaucracies is a mark of appropriate worldly wisdom or just sheer worldliness that privileges elites at the expense of others.

In regard to the ever present temptation to rationalize, I remember historian James Bratt speaking of the "seductive powers of economies of scale" that tempt evangelical institutions to think that "bigger is better." He also warned of economic necessity being turned into evangelical virtue: Cooperating with other groups merely to survive becomes a splendid venture of ecumenical goodwill, or refusing to file proper tax information is defended as keeping God's money out of the hands of worldly powers.[8]

One can observe theology being used to justify all sorts of economic situations and decisions. But, as theologian John Mulder has argued, it is not equally good theology in each case.[9] Sometimes, of course, the theology is sheer hypocrisy. Often, however, the theological ideas used to consider money are sound enough, but there are not enough of them—not enough to provide theological and ethical balance and thus prevent easy and extreme decisions. The typical evangelical impulse toward pragmatism, evangelism, and activism and away from systematic theological reflection has not served evangelicalism well in this respect.[10]

8. Conference on "Evangelicals and Finances," Institute for the Study of American Evangelicals, Naperville, Illinois, 3 December 1998, author's notes.
9. John M. Mulder, "Faith and Money: Theological Reflections on Financing American Religion," in *Financing American Religion*, 157–68.
10. Mark A. Noll, *The Scandal of the Evangelical Mind* (Grand Rapids: Eerdmans, 1994).

A related dynamic in evangelical history has been the invocation of secular wisdom to solve Christian financial disputes. "Each generation should pay its own debts" has justified a refusal to take out long-term loans, while "each generation should pay its own way" has warranted a refusal to seek endowment funds. Both of these proverbs have been solemnly intoned as if they were Proverbs. Again, the fundamental question appears concerning which values, which wisdom, even which language Christians have used to think about and therefore make use of money.

Finally, all of these themes need to be seen in the light of the **Christian story** of creation, fall, redemption, and consummation. Where have we been, where are we now, and where are we going? Jesus frequently discusses money as if there are two realms distinguished both spatially (earth and heaven) and chronologically (this world and the next). His consistent message is that we need to view money and make financial decisions with this twofold reality in mind. How are this cosmology and this teleology, as it were, to be understood and applied in our day?

If Christ is returning imminently to establish an entirely new heaven and earth upon the eradication of the current cosmos, investing in long-term projects would be a waste of valuable and urgently needed resources. If instead there is to be a great deal of continuity between this world and the new earth to be inaugurated, then some kinds of investments in, say, environmental stewardship are indeed justified in the long haul. We would be cooperating with God in his ongoing project of redeeming the planet. What, then, is the church's **mission** in the world in the light of this vast story? Is it primarily evangelism, justice seeking, charity to the needy, worship, living out the values of the kingdom of God as "proleptic community," or perhaps some combination of these?

Answering such questions brings to the fore the question of **value** and what counts as success. According to what standard does an individual believer and a Christian organization rightly measure success in the service of God? What is, in short, the good life? Money is an all-too-convenient symbol, whether in terms of income, expenditure, savings, or investments. This individual is blessed by God: One can ascertain this by how much money she has—or has given away. That organization is failing to please God: One can tell by its small donor base—or by its sponsorship by rich (and therefore suspect) Christians. Where does the sense of value and worth (as in "net worth" or "worthy service") come from for Christians?

Money is a complicated symbol psychologically, and it is bound up with a daunting range of theological themes.[11] It is hardly surprising, therefore, that evangelicals have disagreed with one another over it and have even found it difficult to treat it consistently. Whatever the theological tradition and conviction, however, it seems fair to suggest at least that Christians should think and act in regard to money in a way consistent with their convictions about fundamental theological themes. Indeed, a well-formed theology should act as a sort of razor: Properly honed, it should help Christians, whether individuals or institutions, make decisions about money.

Ironically, one can look at the money/theology relationship the other way. In doing so, one can claim dominical authority for concluding that theology, whether well formed or not, has indeed affected evangelical decisions about money. As one observes how North American evangelicals have raised, spent, and thought about money in history, one sees what Christ himself encouraged one to see: Where our treasure has been, there our hearts—and minds—have been also.[12]

---

11. For recent reflections by a Christian psychologist, see David G. Benner, *Money Madness and Financial Freedom* (Calgary: Detselig, 1996).

12. See Larry Eskridge and Mark A. Noll, eds., *More Money, More Ministry: Money and Evangelicals in Recent North American History* (Grand Rapids: Eerdmans, 2000); cf. Clapp, *Consuming Passion;* and Chaves and Miller, *Financing American Religion.*

6

The Christian Church in the New Dark Age

Illiteracy, Aliteracy, and the Word of God

Evangelicals at their best are realists who take sin and evil as seriously as the Bible does. Evangelicals—not to put too fine a point on it—expect trouble. And they distrust anyone who suggests that life is easy, the way is smooth, and happy days are here again. So let me say this instead: A new Dark Age is advancing upon us, and we had better recognize it and deal with it.

It is a strange Dark Age, to be sure, for it is very well illuminated. Television screens at home glow all day and much of the night, as do computer screens at work and in our home offices. Instead of the flickering golden candlelight thrown off by medieval tapers, our civilization is lit by the bluish light of the cathode-ray tube, supplemented by fluorescent bulbs inside and halogen streetlights and neon signs outside.

It is a strange Dark Age in another respect as well, for the previous Dark Age got its name from the way the lamp of culture burned low. Tribal warfare wracked Europe for centuries after the decline of the Roman Empire. It was pacified only briefly by Charlemagne (ca. 800) and then resumed after his death. Most people counted themselves fortunate to survive on the poor agriculture of the era, hoping not to be called into battle because of some foolish knight's quest or to have to defend their farms against marauders. Formal learning of even an elementary level was restricted to an elite of clergy and nobility. Numerous reforming church councils of this era sought to end the common practice of ordaining priests who could not read and could remember only snatches of Latin in which to say a basic mass. And superstition and magic were the staples of folk religion. Indeed, some scholars nowadays believe that a majority of the European population was converted to one or another form of mainstream Christianity only in the sixteenth century, at the end of the Middle Ages, when Protestant and Catholic reformers competed for the allegiance of the continent.[1] Before this, in the supposedly Christian Middle Ages, Christianity was a thin veneer imposed—usually by force of arms and the rewards of social status—on the entrenched folkways of the various European tribes.

These various dimensions of cultural darkness, furthermore, were interrelated. Economic development could not take place without political stability, while political stability could not be won until victorious powers possessed the resources to maintain peace in conquered lands. Economic and political chaos, furthermore, meant conditions that made it impossible for culture to flourish: No one reads if he must farm; no one attends school unless his family can afford to do without his labor; no one paints or composes or writes if there is no money for paint or paper or ink. In addition, it is difficult to be enthusiastic about Christianity when the local holy man is (as he often was in the early Middle Ages) ignorant, lazy, decidedly unholy, and no more emancipated from magic and superstition than you.

In North America today, we see that things are much, much different—aren't they? Yes, our economy is under stress, and many do not have what we would call adequate subsistence. But most of us do. It is normal in the United States and in Canada, in a way that medievals could scarcely have dreamed of, to go to bed without hunger, while taking for granted a refrigerator and cupboard filled with food for the morrow. Nor is Canada or the United States currently in a large-scale war, although conflict with Islamic terrorists looms ominously as a parallel with medieval European struggles with Islamic empires around the Mediterranean. Internally we are dismayed in Canada by

1. I have in mind here such arguments as those of Jean Delumeau, *Catholicism between Luther and Voltaire: A New View of the Counter-Reformation*, trans. Jeremy Moiser (London: Burns & Oates; Philadelphia: Westminster, 1977 [French 1971]).

the hot tempers flaring about the threat of Quebec's secession and the vexing claims of aboriginal peoples, and in the United States by the agonizing legacy of racism and the increasing tensions surrounding Latino immigration, but few of us contemplate civil war outside our nightmares. We sleep soundly in secure houses and do not fear our neighbors, nor do we keep watchful vigil, shotgun in hand, every time an unfamiliar car comes down the street or a stranger passes by the house.

In such security and prosperity, our culture then flourishes, doesn't it? Plays in theaters, music in concert halls, stores crammed full of CDs and DVDs, televisions going night and day, books stuffing bookstore shelves and piled in discount bins, museums and galleries in every major center and many smaller ones as well. Christianity itself, while it has fallen in general public esteem in Canada since the Second World War, nonetheless continues to attract a quarter of the population of that country to worship every Sunday; continues to produce its own books, magazines, videos, musical recordings, and conferences; continues to play an important enough role in culture that news media feature it from time to time. All of this is true in greater proportions in the United States. In sum, isn't this, so to speak, a Bright Age?

I am still too young to have earned the privilege of curmudgeonhood, but I am not too young to fear for our society and for the Christian church in our society. I should like to express some of that fear by reference to the fears expressed by three other voices.

The first voice is that of Neil Postman, professor of communications at New York University and a well-known pundit on the effects of technology on American culture—and, by implication, on modern cultures everywhere. In several books and many essays, notably *Technopoly*, *Conscientious Objections*, and especially *Amusing Ourselves to Death*, Postman proves to be a prophet, a carrier of a simple message that he reiterates a hundred different ways: We are in a time of profound change, especially in *technology*, and even more particularly in *communications* technology. This change, which is unprecedented in the history of our civilization in its scope and its speed, is changing the way we live. Indeed, it is changing the way we live so profoundly and so quickly that we, while we may sense that something is going on, scarcely can discern what it is, let alone know how to respond.[2]

Television, above all, is the medium of this change. Most of us think of it as a medium of news and entertainment. But Postman maintains, in tones reminiscent of his mentor Marshall McLuhan, that the medium changes the news and entertainment, and thus it changes our perception of the world through that news and entertainment. It is not just that television news, for instance, is more interesting to absorb than newspaper news. It is *different news.*

Postman suggests that if one were to transcribe all the words spoken on a typical half hour television newscast, they would scarcely fill a single page of newsprint. Yes, the "visuals" might be worth a few thousand more words. Or maybe not. Often the images on TV only dramatize and illustrate information that is already conveyed by the voiced-over commentary of the reporter. Yet it costs someone half an hour to take in this news—plus all the sponsoring commercials, of course—rather than the relatively few minutes it would take to read much more information in the newspaper.

Furthermore, there is something deeply controlling about TV news. You must watch it in the order that some producer wants you to view it. Unlike a newspaper, in which you can pick out your favorite sections first and then digest however much else of the newspaper it suits you to read, a news broadcast must be watched just as it is given. And forget about folding up the last ten minutes of the broadcast, tucking it under your arm, and heading off to the bus to view it later! True, you could videotape it for viewing at some other time—but you won't, will you?

But how is this *different news?* It is less news, yes. And it is news heavily interpreted by producers, yes. But is it different? It is different precisely in the fact that images are what drive TV, including news—not informational content and certainly not words per se. If a story has excellent visuals, it will run

2. Neil Postman, *Amusing Ourselves to Death: Public Discourse in the Age of Show Business* (New York: Penguin, 1985); idem, *Conscientious Objections: Stirring Up Trouble about Language, Technology, and Education* (New York: Vintage, 1988); and idem, *Technopoly: The Surrender of Culture to Technology* (New York: Vintage, 1992).

prominently; if it doesn't, it probably won't. That's because TV news nowadays is more about entertainment than about public service. If the news ever gets boring, you'll switch channels. (Remote controls themselves have greatly influenced television programming: Witness the "sideways squeeze" at the end of most programs that allows the network to keep you hooked while the credits roll.) And images arrest the attention of more of us, even intelligent ones of us, than mere information does. Few of us really prefer to view talking heads mulling over the American State of the Union Address or the Canadian Speech from the Throne rather than gripping footage of the latest highway accident, even though the former subjects are far more important and relevant to all of us than the latter.

Furthermore, visuals often convey something *different*. A reporter might tell us that So-and-So appeared today for his trial—no big deal, a completely impartial matter of fact. But if the visuals are shot by a mobile camera tracking the individual from his car, down the sidewalk, and into the courthouse with the usual bumping along the way, we now just *know* that this guy is guilty! He's trying to escape us, isn't he? A reporter might tell us that fully 1 percent of a population is affected by this or that and imply that this is a big deal. But if we are then shown a huge pie chart with 99 percent of it white and only a sliver colored, say, light green, the information may be exactly correct, but it may seem to *mean* something else.

Television and other newer technologies affect our communication in other ways as well. It is a cliché, but no less important for that, that our political leaders strive in their public communications for the punchy sound bite that will get them on the evening broadcast. Because television serves up only tiny little packets of information for fear of boring viewers (or confusing them, which many people sense as simply boredom!), it tightly restricts this tremendously popular conduit through which politicians—or anyone else—can get across their messages. (I was interviewed by ABC News on the complicated question of why candidates were referring to religion so much in the presidential campaign of 2000. After several takes in which I boiled my point down as far as I could, I was encouraged to try harder: "That was fine, Dr. Stackhouse, but it was still about thirty-nine seconds. We need about eighteen.") We know, but perhaps still forget while we're watching, that the television pipe is extremely small, and so the message must be reduced to fit it.

An entire campaign for election to the presidency of the United States, and a successful one, was waged on one phrase: "It's Morning in America" (Reagan 1984). Tellingly, that one phrase was promoted over and over again on television commercials that featured winsome images from the lexicon of classic Americana: Old Glory being raised, grandparents cuddling children, a soldier hugging his girlfriend, a farmer plowing his field at sunset. A vacuous phrase matched with good visuals did much of the job. The next presidential election (Bush 1988) was won largely with another catchy slogan: "Read my lips: no new taxes." Now, the American presidency is the most important office on earth, responsible for the most complex political organism the world has ever seen. And yet all that its leaders seem to be able to communicate to the electorate are the contents of bumper stickers.

A similar phenomenon has occurred on the Internet. I use electronic mail every working day, and it is a wonderful tool: communication over many miles at low cost. But I don't write letters anymore. I quickly dash off "posts" or "emails." The entire genre of correspondence has changed: short, blunt, rushed. And sometimes dangerously unclear: How many of us have had to invest considerable time in putting out relational fires started by someone who misunderstood the tone and intention of someone else's email?

Even scholars now pay so little attention to the evocative dimension of their writing on the net that an entire visual vocabulary has had to be devised. The so-called emoticons make little faces out of computer keystrokes to communicate the emotional tone of the sentence. But whatever did writers do to convey this in the past—like, a decade ago? They wrote carefully, that's what they did. They paid attention to the craft of writing and sought to use just the right words to get their point across. We're too busy for that now.

This is what Postman means by his wonderful phrase "public discourse in an age of show business." And here's my final example, inspired by his message. When I go to scholarly meetings, I read over the program to decide which sessions I will attend. What has impressed me about a number of such meetings in the last several years is the increase of titles that include some reference to popular culture—and usually a television program, movie, or advertising slogan—in the title. The Nike shoe company's "Just do it" slogan enjoyed a huge success in the 1990s, but lyrics from rap songs, phrases from McDonald's commercials, and jokes by David Letterman or Jay Leno are all fair game.

Presumably, the scholars who employ such devices are showing us that they are hip, *au courant,* and therefore both interesting and important. What one sees in a previous generation, even in popular writing such as that of C. S. Lewis, H. L. Mencken, or George Grant, are frequent allusions to an entirely different set of cultural commonplaces: the Greek and Roman classics, Shakespeare, the English and American novels of the nineteenth century, and, above all, the Bible. The point I am making here is one already made by cultural critics such as E. D. Hirsch in books such as his *Cultural Literacy: What Every American Needs to Know.*[3] But my illustration points to the reality, I think, that even *scholars* don't know or care about these allusions anymore. They keep up with popular movies and television but don't know *King Lear* from *Macbeth.* They know who's hot and who's not in Hollywood but couldn't tell King David from David Copperfield. If you want to relate to people today, even in an academic society, apparently you have to reach out to the world of popular entertainment.

The world of television, movies, and pop music is discussed by the second voice, the chorus of authors who together wrote *Dancing in the Dark: Youth, Popular Culture, and the Electronic Media.*[4] In this book, six concerned Christian scholars examine the youth culture of the United States and warn us of the changes wrought by the interaction of this culture with the electronic media. One of the most important things they tell us is that our youth get their cues today not primarily from their parents (as parents already know!) and not primarily from their churches (as everybody already knows!) but also not primarily

3. E. D. Hirsch, *Cultural Literacy: What Every American Needs to Know* (Boston: Houghton Mifflin, 1987).
4. Quentin Schultze et al., *Dancing in the Dark: Youth, Popular Culture, and the Electronic Media* (Grand Rapids: Eerdmans, 1991).

from their peers, at least not in the sense of a local group. Instead, what peer pressure they feel comes in the form of conformity to fashions, tastes, and trends that in fact originate far away from the local peer group: in Hollywood, New York, Nashville, and other generators of popular culture.

Youth culture is now a national—really, an international—phenomenon, not a local one, let alone a neighborhood one. Kids at high schools in Toronto dress the same as kids in high schools in Halifax, Montreal, Winnipeg, and Vancouver. They also dress the same as kids in Chicago, Miami, and Dallas—except perhaps for local adjustments (cowboy boots in Dallas) or ethnic differences (black or Latino fashions in Chicago and Miami—but then black and Hispanic kids dress the same in Los Angeles or Newark!). The music is the same, and the talk is the same, with Southern California being the main manufacturer of new language, rivaled only by black or Latino neighborhoods in Chicago and New York.

The electronic web of television, movies, and music—and the wedding of those three technologies to produce the new genre of music videos—is the primary source of "what's goin' on" and "what's yesterday." Here is where kids learn what it means to be a man or a woman. Here is where kids learn what it means to be a friend or an enemy. Here is where kids learn what it means to be religious, patriotic, loyal, or clever. Here is where kids learn what it means to succeed.

Over his career, the late Allan Bloom taught at some of the finest universities in the world. A decade ago, this is what he observed among his students at the University of Chicago:

> Our students have lost the practice of and the taste for reading. They have not learned how to read, nor do they have the expectation of delight or improvement from reading. . . .
>
> When I first noticed the decline in reading during the late sixties, I began asking my large introductory classes, and any other group of younger students to which I spoke, what books really count for them. Most are silent, puzzled by the question. The notion of books as companions is foreign to them.[5]

5. Allan Bloom, *The Closing of the American Mind: How Higher Education Has Failed Democracy and Impoverished the Souls of Today's Students* (New York: Simon & Schuster, 1987), 62.

Another college teacher cautions us against plunking down a book in front of our glazed-eyed teenagers. Such nonreaders may not only ignore the book but may actually resent it—and us. "They didn't get it," he writes of one of his classes that had struggled with what, to him, was a rather elementary story. "And their not getting it angered them, and they expressed their anger by drawing around themselves a cowl of ill-tempered apathy."[6] We have here a definite echo of the Master's warning about casting pearls before swine. We have to educate people to appreciate that jewels are not immediately useful things—not edible or comfortable or pleasurable—but they are valuable to the discerning eye and cultivated mind. It takes civilization to appreciate them, as it does to read books well.

Much of this—perhaps all of it—we all already know. But before we turn to the question of response (and we will, since evangelicals, for all our appreciation of the dark side of things, historically have been active in responding to it with Christian energy, determination, and skill), let us hear one more voice that focuses our attention on one aspect of this daunting cultural reality. In some ways this voice seems preoccupied with a hilariously secondary problem, like someone who wails about the disorder of the deck chairs as the deck of the Titanic continues to slant. But let us hear him for a few minutes anyhow and see if he can help us even a bit as we make our way in the darkness lit up by MuchMusic and MTV.

Sven Birkerts writes about "the fate of reading in an electronic age" in his collection of essays entitled *The Gutenberg Elegies.* Birkerts does not focus on the evil content of television or the movies. He does not worry primarily about pornography on music videos or the Internet. Bad as those problems undoubtedly are, he notices something else about the electronic media. Like Postman and McLuhan and other prophets of the electronic age, Birkerts is interested in the medium of literature as much as he is in the contents of it, and he finds that electronic media change the way we perceive and think about the world.

According to Birkerts, we see things in bits and pieces, with no overarching story or philosophy to make sense of the rush of

6. Sven Birkerts, *The Gutenberg Elegies: The Fate of Reading in an Electronic Age* (New York: Fawcett Columbine, 1994), 18.

data we receive. We do not see narrative, story line, plot, continuity. We see a news story, then another one that is completely unrelated, and then a commercial that has nothing to do with either. In fact, as Postman famously titled one of his own essays on the subject, the only connection a newscaster provides between the foregoing news stories and the upcoming commercial is no connection at all: "Now . . . this." And remember that Postman is citing from the news—you know, the putatively serious, intellectual part of TV—not the entertainment that washes over us without us thinking much about it.

Indeed, the logic of Birkerts, Postman, and company would seem to be that it is better for our minds, given the unpleasant choice, to read a trashy novel than to watch the same trashy content on TV, for even plowing through Harold Robbins or Robert Ludlum or a Harlequin romance requires the exercise, at least mildly, of intellectual skills and habits of mind that are hardly required when sitting in front of the TV set.

What skills? The skill of hearing an author's voice and making sense of it. The skill of decoding words on a page and creating a world in your mind, of manufacturing locations and costumes and faces and voices. And the skill of stopping and considering and evaluating what one reads and then moving on.

What habits? The habit of sitting still and carefully submitting to an author's direction, at the author's pace. The habit of shutting out the rest of the world and slipping into what Birkerts calls "deep time," the suspended consciousness of what we call the absorbed reader. The habit of engaging the author with critical attention, sometimes explicitly agreeing or disagreeing, perhaps with mutters under one's breath. And the habit of then releasing oneself from the author's direction by pausing, digressing, letting a train of thought move out of the station of the book at hand and riding it to new ideas or revisiting old ones, only later to return to the station and resume the book.

In some ways, our modern connections through the media help us to see the world better. We know more about other lands and peoples than we did in the past, through instantaneous, long-distance communication. But in some ways we also see it worse. We know less about ourselves, and particularly our histories, than we did even a generation or two ago.

We have no sense of place and time, no standpoint from which to consider the variety of alternative values, ideas, traditions, and habits of others. We don't know who we are, so we have trouble understanding anyone else.

A final observation prompted by Birkerts, Postman, and others may seem obvious, but it points to a reality nonetheless insidious. The electronic media take up space, time, and money that could be devoted—and, until recently, were devoted—to other activities, especially to reading.[7] There isn't time in a day or a week to indulge in them all. So what do we choose after a day's work and the kids are finally quiet? A book, particularly one that demands the work of patient interpretation and active imagination? Or the hockey game? A popular television drama? Or surfing the Internet?

Now, someone might respond that we do in fact read a lot nowadays. Aren't there more books and magazines and web sites and instruction manuals than ever? How can one bemoan a supposed loss of reading in the information age?

One bemoans it in at least two respects. First, many of us do not, in fact, read much or often. Do I need to furnish statistics for this unstartling claim? Even among people with good formal education, reading time is given short shrift: Weeks, even months, slide by with newspapers scanned, magazines given a glance or two, and only *TV Guide* consulted regularly.

The second respect in which one can deplore the state of reading is by observing that there is reading and there is reading and there is reading, and we tend to read only at the first two levels. The great critic George Steiner speaks first of reading for distraction—the airport book, the thriller, the romance. Steiner speaks second of reading for information—whether office files, the *Wall Street Journal,* recipes, instructions, self-help books, and so on.[8] The third level is the deep reading of Birkerts, the "slow reading" of James Sire.[9] This is the reading that does not just "use" a book but converses with it, treating it with

7. Postman, *Technopoly,* 16.

8. See George Steiner, "The Uncommon Reader," in his *No Passion Spent: Essays 1978–1995* (New Haven and London: Yale University Press, 1996), 1–19.

9. James W. Sire, *How to Read Slowly: A Christian Guide to Reading with the Mind* (Downers Grove, Ill.: InterVarsity, 1978).

respect as a companion—as Bloom suggests. This is the reading that shapes minds and souls, reading that is truly of and in the spirit. Poetry obviously requires this kind of reading. Drama does too. Essays, novels, and, above all, Scripture require it: It is *this* reading that is vanishing all around us.

People don't read, and we forget how to read well or never learn. Indeed, one of the most shocking examples of this phenomenon can be furnished immediately in any group of Christians. Produce a paragraph of Scripture (even a relatively straightforward teaching passage from the epistles), and ask each person to articulate just the main point of that paragraph in one sentence. Then stand back and watch the chaos. People cannot read with discipline, with attention, with submission to the text. They read for use or for entertainment ("Here's what I think is interesting" or "Here's what it means to me") but not for real engagement with another mind ("Here's what it says—and now I'll have to think about it").

So what can we North American evangelicals do? We must meet at least three conditions if we are to be useful in this growing crisis. First, we have to be in touch—indeed, in friendly and continuous contact—with other Christians so that the way is open for the giving and receiving of blessing. If Presbyterians and Episcopalians maintain an aloofness from, say, Pentecostals or Mennonites, then they will not think to share the blessing of their heritage, will not want to share their blessing, and will be unable to share their blessing. Just as many of us have been roused by Pentecostal enthusiasm in our worship and prodded by Anabaptist witness in our attitudes toward wealth and war, so many of us need to be instructed by the Reformed, Anglican, and other traditions of Christianity that have preserved a heritage of serious intellectual labor.

Second, for the intellectually minded among evangelicals to bring to the larger church their rich heritage of Christian thought, they need to be thoroughly Christian. By this I mean that they had better have not only well-furnished minds but also warm hearts and active hands. Cold intellectualism is a gift to no one, but an able mind in concert with a passionate heart and helping hands has much to offer. Presbyterians in the past were unabashed revivalists. Lutherans in the past wrote some of the church's great hymns and prayers. Anglicans in the past led the way in helping the poor, the neglected, the oppressed, and the ignorant. These well-balanced traditions must be recovered and adapted to the needs of our day.

Some of us today might be uncomfortable with other Christians' expressions of piety, whether, say, charismatic or Catholic. But we had better have our own piety in working order, so to speak, so we do not disqualify ourselves from speaking to others. Some of us inclined toward the life of the mind might be uncomfortable with the activism of some Christians in mass evangelism or social action. But we had better have our own ministry to the needy so we do not disqualify ourselves from speaking to others out of our ivory towers.

Third, intellectually interested evangelicals need, in fact, to be thinking. We need to carry on the heritage of Christian thought with active programs of Christian thought today. We need to read, and read well and often. We need to shut off the TV, establish a quiet place with a good light and a comfortable chair, with the stereo silent and the phone on the answering machine, and get to the blessed labor of deep reading. If nothing else, we need to take fifteen to twenty minutes each evening, if only before bed, and read: We won't miss the sleep, but at this pace we will read another book a month.

Such evangelicals also need to demand from their preachers learned sermons, not sermons with showy references and clever allusions, but sermons that bear the fruit of wide and deep reading. We also need to provide our pastors with the time, books, and stimulation of conferences and summer schools that are necessary to produce such vital blessings. Furthermore, we need to demand from our leaders guidance as to what we ought to be reading as laypeople and how we can choose among the welter of books and magazines available what will be most helpful. We also need to demand such guidance of Christian booksellers, who all too often seem to hire staff because they are friends or relatives of the owners, not because they actually are "book people" who can recommend reading the way any good car salesman can recommend a car, or any good clothing saleswoman can recommend a dress.

Perhaps most radically, churches need to become places in which people once again are trained to read. We need much better training than we usually get as to how to read the Bible properly and profitably, but we also need teaching as to how to read the newspaper, how to select and read contemporary fiction and essays, how to read poetry and drama and biography and science and theology. The Sunday school was begun a century ago, not to teach Christian children the basics of the faith but to teach illiterate street kids how to read. I fear we now need to provide such teaching again for all who will come, adults as well as children.

George Steiner has warned us in an ominous prophecy: "What about reading in the old, archaic, private, silent sense? This may become as specialized a skill and avocation as it was in the scriptoria and libraries of the monasteries during the so-called Dark Ages."[10] The church had to hold up the lamp of learning during those terrible times. The church since then has brought this lamp to cultures around the world, whose languages were reduced to writing and whose first books were produced by missionaries intent on sharing the Word of God with them. The church today and in the future will have to lift this lamp high amid fellow Christians who are either illiterate (cannot read) or aliterate (can read but do not) and amid what may be the twilight—or at least *a* twilight—of our civilization.

10. Quoted from the R. R. Bowker memorial lecture, without further reference, in Postman, *Conscientious Objections*, 55.

7

A "Paradigm Case"

Billy Graham and the Nature of Conversion

There can be little doubt that the figure of Christian evangelist Billy Graham (1918–) looms large over the landscape of American religion. The preacher from the backwoods of North Carolina is now easily the most famous, widely traveled, and acclaimed preacher in history. He has toured five continents, speaking in huge churches and stadiums to record audiences. He penetrated the Iron Curtain before it was torn in the late 1980s, adding the Second World to his itinerary, which had included most of the First and Third Worlds already. And he has made adroit use of the most modern communication technology, including best-selling books, *Decision* magazine (which has long enjoyed the highest circulation of any religious periodical in North America), television specials, a popular newspaper column, a movie studio, and a mail-handling operation in the Minneapolis headquarters so renowned for volume and efficiency that experts from Madison Avenue and both major American political parties have studied it to improve their own.

So conspicuous a figure, one who has enjoyed the limelight since the famous Los Angeles crusade of 1949 that launched him into national prominence, naturally has attracted tremendous attention from journalists and scholars. Sociologists of conversion have been especially active among the latter, with studies of Graham crusades now going back more than thirty years.[1] What has trammeled several of these studies, however, and therefore the use of Graham crusades as putative "paradigm cases" of conversion, is the lack of serious attention to Graham's own understanding of conversion and to his interpretation of what goes on in his meetings. Consideration of Graham's views leads to a more nuanced and complex conception—ironically, that is, to a better paradigm—of the key sociological terms *conversion* and *commitment*.[2]

Conversion according to Billy Graham

Billy Graham has received a great deal of criticism through the years, and two main types have emerged regarding conversion. The first, and the most popular especially among those unfamiliar with Graham, is that his evangelistic meetings, known as crusades, are too efficient in producing converts. The slick advertising blitz before and during the meetings, the program featuring celebrities (usually athletes, politicians, or singers), the mass choir (sometimes numbering in the thousands), the tried-and-true order of service with predictable emotional highs and lows, and the formulaic preaching of Graham himself all lead inexorably to hun-

1. K. Lang and G. E. Lang, "Decisions for Christ: Billy Graham in New York City," in *Identity and Anxiety*, ed. M. Stein et al. (New York: Free Press, 1960), 415–27; F. L. Whitam, "Revivalism as Institutionalized Behavior: An Analysis of the Social Base of a Billy Graham Crusade," *Social Science Quarterly* 49 (1968): 115–27; Weldon T. Johnson, "The Religious Crusade: Revival or Ritual?" *American Journal of Sociology* 76 (1971): 873–90; Donald A. Clelland and Thomas C. Hood, "In the Company of the Converted: Characteristics of a Billy Graham Crusade Audience," *Sociological Analysis* 35 (1974): 45–56; R. C. Wimberley et al., "Conversion in a Billy Graham Crusade: Spontaneous Event or Ritual Performance," *Sociological Quarterly* 16 (1975): 162–70; and Norris R. Johnson et al., "Attendance at a Billy Graham Crusade: A Resource Mobilization Approach," *Sociological Analysis* 45 (1984): 383–92.

2. I am following Thomas Kuhn in using "paradigm" in the sense of an overarching intellectual model or framework, while recognizing that considerable controversy has attended Kuhn's use of this word (Thomas S. Kuhn, *The Structure of Scientific Revolutions*, 2d ed. [1962; reprint, Chicago: University of Chicago Press, 1970]). For a helpful summary of sociological scholarship regarding conversion, see Lewis R. Rambo, *Understanding Religious Conversion* (New Haven/London: Yale University Press, 1993).

dreds of mass-produced, superficial "conversion experiences."[3] These experiences are manufactured with regard neither for the subsequent spiritual development of these people nor for their integration into local churches that will care for them long after the Graham show has left town.[4]

The other sort of criticism, paradoxically, is that the Graham crusades are not efficient enough. In spite of the impressive crowd size, they produce relatively few real converts among those from unchurched backgrounds, and among these, few actually join churches and stick with their "Graham crusade decision."[5]

These criticisms can be raised fairly regardless of one's actual agreement with Graham's doctrine and his desire to see people converted to evangelical Christianity. What they both come down to is a fundamental question: Is the mass-evangelism approach of Graham and his team an effective means to the desired end? To answer this question, however, we must pose a prior one: What *is* the desired end? What is, in fact, conversion as Graham understands it?

The Anglo-American evangelical tradition, reaching back to the eighteenth-century revivals under the Wesleys in England and Jonathan Edwards in America, asserts that authentic Christianity entails a personal—we could now say "existential"—experience and appropriation of the Christian faith. More than this, historic evangelicalism declares that Christians fundamentally are not to be identified as those

3. Lewis R. Rambo, "Current Research on Religious Conversion," *Religious Studies Review* 8 (1984): 146–59; David A. Snow and Richard Machalek, "The Sociology of Conversion," *Annual Review of Sociology* 10 (1984): 167–90; and Irwin R. Barker and Raymond F. Currie, "Do Converts Always Make the Most Committed Christians?" *Journal for the Scientific Study of Religion* 24 (1985): 305–13.

4. Reinhold Niebuhr, "Proposal to Billy Graham," *The Christian Century* 73 (1956): 921–22; cf. Whitam, "Revivalism."

5. So William G. McLoughlin, Jr.'s summary: "The two most frequent complaints made against Billy Graham are the same ones which have been leveled against all professional evangelists: They are that his converts do not stick and that as his organization increases its size and scope it tends to become increasingly commercial in character" (*Billy Graham: Revivalist in a Secular Age* [New York: Ronald Press, 1960], 174). And for one other example, see the very restricted study by Johnson, "Religious Crusade."

who practice the Christian religion per se but as those who
have spiritually met Jesus Christ and have gratefully entered
into a covenant of love with him. Christians are those who
have passed over from the darkness of inherited, or original,
sin and alienation from God into the light of forgiveness and
reconciliation with God. This "passing over" comes as they
are "born again," given new life in Christ in succession to
their old existence of self-centeredness and spiritual death.
Conversion, then, quite straightforwardly means "a change
of state," particularly in this case a change of mind (so the
Greek *metanoia*).

The stereotype many of us inherit from nineteenth-century camp meetings and twentieth-century mass rallies is
that evangelicals believe in a onetime, precisely datable conversion experience. This is exactly the sort of thing one might
presume (and many have claimed) is engendered by Graham
crusades. But the evangelical tradition, in fact, has posed
more than one answer on this point. Many prominent leaders through the centuries have defended the idea that there
is a variety of conversion "trajectories," with some centering
on a particular crisis experience and others characterized by
a process of growing acquaintance with and trust in Jesus
Christ.[6]

Graham, at least from his earliest writing, has belonged to the
latter category of those teaching more than one "paradigm" of
conversion. In 1953, in his first best-selling book, Graham set out
how he believed men and women could find *Peace with God:*

6. Jerald C. Brauer, "Conversion: From Puritanism to Revivalism," *Journal
of Religion* 58 (1978): 227–43; Bill J. Leonard, "Getting Saved in America: Conversion Event in a Pluralistic Culture," *Review and Expositor* 82 (winter 1985):
111–27; cf. John Lofland and Norman Skonovd, "Conversion Motifs," *Journal
for the Scientific Study of Religion* 20 (1981): 373–85; and Brock Kilbourne and
James T. Richardson, "Paradigm Conflict, Types of Conversion, and Conversion Theories," *Sociological Analysis* 50 (1989): 1–21. Many evangelical heroes,
such as Martin Luther, John Calvin, John Wesley, and C. S. Lewis, did not have
a "one-time" conversion experience. Indeed, regarding the first three examples, there has been a long-standing discussion among historians and theologians precisely about the nature and process of their evangelical conversions.
Concerning the fourth, see Ralph C. Wood, "On the Long Road Back to Christianity," *The Christian Century* 108 (20–27 November 1991): 1096–101.

Not all conversions come as a sudden, brilliant flash of soul illumination that we call a crisis conversion. There are many others
that are accomplished only after a long and difficult conflict
with the inner motives of the person. With others, conversion
comes as the climactic moment of a long period of gradual conviction of their need and revelation of the plan of salvation. This
prolonged process results in conscious acceptance of Christ as
personal Savior and in the yielding of life to Him.

We may say, therefore, that conversion can be an instantaneous event, a crisis in which the person receives a clear revelation of the love of God; or it can be a gradual unfoldment accom-
panied by a climactic moment at the time the line is crossed
between darkness and light, between death and life everlasting.[7]

Graham came by these views through personal experience
as well as through theological study. Three key women in his
life stand as important types in this regard: his mother, his
wife, and his first love. His mother, Morrow Coffey Graham,
insisted that the family attend a Presbyterian church while
young William Franklin Graham, Jr., was growing up. Her
Christian faith was both obvious to and influential on her
firstborn son, but she would later say, "I couldn't tell you the
day or hour when I was converted, but I knew I was born
again."[8]

Graham's wife, Ruth Bell Graham, offered a similar testimony, which Graham himself recounts to make this point.
Ruth grew up in China as the daughter of staunch Presbyterian missionaries. She had been an exemplary young girl,
with a lively and apparently sincere commitment to Christianity, and Graham had first met her as an outstanding
Christian student on the campus of Wheaton College (an
evangelical liberal arts college in the suburbs of Chicago). He
wrote about her later in respect to our present concern: "My
wife, for example, cannot remember the exact day or hour
when she became a Christian, but she is certain that there
was such a moment in her life, a moment when she actually
crossed the line."[9]

7. Billy Graham, *Peace with God* (New York: Permabooks, 1955), 111.
8. Quoted in William Martin, *A Prophet with Honor: The Billy Graham Story*
(New York: William Morrow, 1991), 59.
9. Graham, *Peace with God*, 111.

A third woman, his first serious love as a teenager, was Pauline Presson, and her story serves as an important counterexample. As the young Graham got more and more serious about his Christian faith, going off to attend Bible school and trying out his wings as a fledgling preacher, his high school sweetheart felt more and more left out. Try as she might, she just could not share his burning commitment and saw him increasingly as eccentric and extreme. They broke up.

Graham returned to his hometown of Charlotte, North Carolina, in 1934 at the age of twenty-six to conduct an evangelistic meeting. Presson decided to attend, and, to her own great surprise and his, she came to the front of the church at the end of the service and declared her intention to convert, to "get saved." Yet she did not hang on. Years later, she told a journalist, "I told him that night I'd try, like I had told him other times before. And I did. But I just couldn't do it. It just wasn't in me. Maybe I just loved life itself too much."[10]

The experiences of these three women doubtless shaped Graham's convictions, and these vignettes illustrate his belief that "coming forward" at a meeting, or having a similar conversion experience in some other venue, is not necessarily the point of authentic Christian conversion and commitment. Indeed, his own case serves as a particularly interesting, if not especially unusual, example of both process and crisis.

Graham was raised in a straightforward Christian home, with both parents publicly and privately practicing a typical southern evangelical faith. In typical southern evangelical style, the teenaged Graham went with a friend to some meetings held by a fiery itinerant evangelist, Mordecai Ham. After attending a series of such meetings in which he felt increasingly as if Ham was singling him out as "a grea-a-a-at sinner," he and a friend "walked the sawdust trail."

Graham was not at the time a particularly great sinner, however. In fact, he was rather at a loss initially to demonstrate his supposedly newfound faith, since he had none of the reprehensible habits associated with notorious sin in that

10. Quoted in Marshall Frady, *Billy Graham: A Parable of American Righteousness* (Boston/Toronto: Little, Brown, 1979), 103.

culture, whether dancing, gambling, fornicating, or drinking. So was he really "converted" under Ham, or did he undergo the southern evangelical equivalent of "confirmation" or "bar mitzvah"?

Graham did, to be sure, commit himself to Bible school training and went off after high school graduation to Tennessee for one term and then to Florida for three years. While in Florida, he became convinced of his own lack of spiritual seriousness, particularly when his fiancée, a fellow student, broke off their engagement over just that issue. Walking despondently through the empty Tampa streets night after night, he finally knelt down on the eighteenth green of a golf course near the college and committed his life decisively to God. From then on, he was a highly motivated preacher. Was this conversion number two?

Graham then attended and graduated with a B.A. from Wheaton College. He married Ruth Bell shortly thereafter and began his full-time preaching career, most notably with the brand-new Youth for Christ movement. While in Britain on a tour for that organization, he encountered a spry Welshman named Stephen Olford. Hearing Olford preach on the "filling of the Holy Spirit," Graham came up afterward and exclaimed, "Mr. Olford, I just want to ask you one question—why didn't you give an invitation? Because I'd have been the first one to come forward. You've spoken about something that I haven't got. I want to know the fullness of the Holy Spirit in my life too. I want what you've got."[11]

Olford and Graham then met together for two solid days of Bible study and prayer in a small hotel, and when they emerged, Graham was a changed man. He was "anointed," as Olford would later testify, with the Holy Spirit and more effective than ever before as an evangelist. Was this a third conversion?[12]

Graham himself looks back to his "coming forward" at Mordecai Ham's revival meeting as his initial "decision for Christ," with the subsequent two crises each marking a significant deepen-

11. Quoted in ibid., 170.
12. These three events are described in the two most recent full-length biographies by Frady, *Billy Graham*, and Martin, *Prophet with Honor*. They, too, raise the issue of several "crises" in Graham's early spiritual development.

ing of his religious commitment.[13] None of these three experiences marks a radical "conversion" from one life pattern to another. Graham's own spiritual journey, then, joins the testimonies of significant women in his life to confirm his conception of what it means to be born again, to have peace with God, to be, as revivalists from an earlier time would put it, "soundly converted."[14]

God must do the work of conversion, of renewal, in the heart. That is first, and Graham routinely answers the question, "How many people have you converted?" with the answer, "Not one. God does the converting."[15]

On the other hand, Graham simultaneously stresses that God works in the heart only with the consent, indeed only with the invitation, of the person himself or herself. The convert, therefore, must be a seeker, must make the commitment to change his or her ultimate allegiances and way of life, and must follow through in these respects in the company of like-minded persons. His own work as an evangelist, therefore, is simply to provide opportunity for the seeker to encounter God's offer of salvation. As Graham has often put it, "I'm just a Western Union boy."

This is an important theological dimension to the ongoing debate in sociology as to whether, and to what extent, conversion is passively received or actively achieved.[16] In the

13. Martin, *Prophet with Honor*, 63–64. It is striking how little extra insight is gathered from Graham's own memoirs: *Billy Graham, Just As I Am: The Autobiography of Billy Graham* (San Francisco: HarperCollins, 1997). He simply does not reflect theologically on the matter of conversion as he does in other works.

14. Graham, *Peace with God;* and idem, *How to Be Born Again* (Waco: Word, 1977).

15. For just one among many examples, see Billy Graham, "Are You Sure You Are Converted?" *Decision* 3 (April 1991): 1.

16. John Lofland and Rodney Stark, "Becoming a World Saver: A Theory of Conversion to a Deviant Perspective," *American Sociological Review* 30 (1965): 862–75; David A. Snow and Richard Machalek, "The Convert as a Social Type," in *Sociological Theory 1983*, ed. R. Collins (San Francisco: Jossey-Bass, 1983), 259–89; idem, "Sociology of Conversion"; James T. Richardson, "The Active vs. Passive Convert: Paradigm Conflict in Conversion/Recruitment Research," *Journal for the Scientific Study of Religion* 24 (1985): 119–236; and Clifford L. Staples and Armand L. Mauss, "Conversion or Commitment: A Reassessment of the Snow and Machalek Approach to the Study of Conversion," *Journal for the Scientific Study of Religion* 26 (1987): 133–47.

former respect, God must do it all since only God can create life, only God can raise the dead, only God can bring spiritual renewal. Yet in the actual experience of the Christian and in the personal appropriation of the divine work of conversion, the subject must himself or herself *do* something, as Graham emphasizes: He or she must accept God's grace and make a commitment to follow Christ as Lord.[17]

The second point Graham's theology of conversion makes clear is that there is indeed a point in the truly Christian person's life at which he or she crosses the line from death to life, from sin to salvation. Since everyone inherits original sin, everyone needs this spiritual transformation that God alone can effect. This belief explains why Graham consistently speaks of conversion in terms of a "line" being "crossed," of an "event" taking place at some point in a Christian's life. The crucial qualifier according to Graham, however, is that it is not for human observers—and sometimes not even for the subject himself or herself—to detect just when that line is crossed. Thus, Graham has produced as examples the testimonies of his mother and his wife.

Third, the Christian life is one of process punctuated by crisis, and the pattern of process and crisis will vary with each individual. Each Christian, however, is in a new life after being born again, and the point is to live that new life, not to rest on some past experience, however dramatic (so Pauline Presson's story). Graham, therefore, does not preach what theologian Dietrich Bonhoeffer memorably castigated as "cheap grace." He very much stands in the classical evangelical tradition of challenging professed Christians to press on in daily, growing obedience to Christ.[18]

Thus, Graham unabashedly appeals to well-churched people in his sermons and books to "come to Christ." He challenges those who believe they are just fine spiritually to reconsider whether they are truly right with God. Some well-churched people, he believes, are simply "social Christians,"

---

17. So Roger A. Straus, "Religious Conversion as a Personal and Collective Accomplishment," *Sociological Analysis* 40 (1979): 162–65.

18. So Peter Berger and Thomas Luckmann: "To have a conversion is nothing much. The real thing is to be able to keep on taking it seriously" (*The Social Construction of Reality* [Garden City, N.Y.: Doubleday, 1967], 158).

mere "professing Christians," not actual friends of Jesus Christ and children of God. One of his favorite sayings is, "Being born in a garage doesn't make you a car." And the mark of true Christianity is not conformity to a supposed evangelical paradigm of having a stereotypical "conversion experience" but whether one is truly, deeply, and completely committed to Christ, trusting him alone for one's salvation and loving and serving him daily. Those who respond positively to this invitation, therefore, are as truly and as radically converted—in the sense of having passed from spiritual death to spiritual life—as any unchurched individual who walks down the aisle with them.[19]

Furthermore, while Graham concentrates on drawing to Christ those who have never yet met him, he also frequently and consistently challenges those who already have done so to renew their acquaintance, to deepen their relationship, and to mature in their faith. Those who respond positively to this challenge of "rededication" he also invites forward at the end of his meetings.

19. McLoughlin, in *Billy Graham*, betrays his failure to comprehend this perspective as he writes, "Graham also makes no distinction between inviting persons to come forward who are nonbelievers and those who are already church members in good standing" (177). Yet McLoughlin also refers to a *Christian Century* article later in his book that reported on the New York crusade of 1957: "While they [those "going forward"] were obviously churchgoers, the correspondent noted that many of them checked 'Acceptance of Christ as Saviour and Lord' on the decision card instead of 'Reaffirmation'" (no author or title, *Christian Century* [12 June 1957]: 725–26; quoted on 185). This phenomenon, of course, is precisely what Graham expects.

Reinhold Niebuhr also caricatures Graham as he characterizes the latter's understanding of evangelism in terms of "creating" a conversion "crisis" ("Proposal to Billy Graham," 921–22).

Indeed, in an otherwise very helpful introduction to Graham, Charles H. Lippy makes the identical "category mistake." Readers by now should be poised to spot the non sequitur: "Crusade analysts have found as well that a significant number of those making a decision for Christ already have formal religious affiliation or former involvement with a religious institution. Thus, the number of converts recorded may exaggerate the number of those making an initial religious commitment" ("Billy Graham," in *Twentieth-Century Shapers of American Popular Religion*, ed. Charles H. Lippy [New York: Greenwood, 1989], 182). Cf. Clelland and Hood, "In the Company of the Converted," 52; and Barker and Currie, "Converts," 306–7.

In this approach of inviting people to make fresh commitments, whether they consider themselves currently Christian or not, Graham stands in the venerable tradition of the revival, for revival, strictly speaking, can come only to those once alive. Revival therefore means, in this understanding, stirring up the already converted to new spiritual vigor. From the days of John Wesley, George Whitefield, and Jonathan Edwards, however, revivalists knew that they were encountering many who were churched but not born again, as well as those who were neither churched nor saved. So they blended the call to the converted with the call to be converted. Thus has Graham issued the same double invitation throughout his career, in full congruence with mainstream evangelical theology.[20]

Conversion at a Billy Graham Crusade

Graham has acted consistently with this understanding of the Christian life and in so doing has provided ample evidence with which one can discount much of the first criticism, namely, that his crusades promote superficial, onetime spiritual experiences.

A sophisticated version of this criticism was raised most trenchantly by the distinguished American theologian Reinhold Niebuhr in the 1950s.[21] Niebuhr, true to his own convictions regarding the importance of the social, political, and therefore deeply corporate nature of Christian mission, flayed Graham in a number of periodicals for what Niebuhr saw to

20. So McLoughlin: "The central purpose of each campaign, of course, is to inaugurate a revival of religion. This means first to stimulate new enthusiasm among current or former church members, and second, to awaken nonbelievers or occasional churchgoers to the need for saving their souls and joining a church" (*Billy Graham*, 175); cf. Brauer, "Conversion"; and Leonard, "Getting Saved." And for a contemporary expression, see David F. Wells, *Turning to God: Biblical Conversion in the Modern World* (Grand Rapids: Baker, 1989).

21. Reinhold Niebuhr, "Editorial Notes," *Christianity and Crisis* 16 (5 March 1956): 18–19; idem, "Literalism, Individualism, and Billy Graham," *The Christian Century* 73 (1956): 640–42; idem, "Proposal to Billy Graham"; idem, "After Comment, the Deluge," *The Christian Century* 74 (1957): 1034–35; and idem, "Differing Views on Billy Graham," *Life* (1 July 1957): 92.

be a naïve and unhelpful focus on individual conversion rather than on social transformation. This criticism, then, was a variation on the theme that Graham cared only for "getting souls born again" rather than proclaiming Christian commitment as concerning whole persons and whole societies here and now for the long term.

One possible rejoinder is that there might have been a division of labor in the kingdom of God that Niebuhr failed to recognize. Niebuhr, after all, if we look at his career from Graham's point of view, was not notably active or successful in converting large numbers of individuals to Christ. That is, as Graham would doubtless put it, evangelism was not Niebuhr's primary calling. Niebuhr, therefore, was correct to pursue what was his calling, but evangelism of this sort was Graham's. Graham, therefore, perhaps cannot be faulted for not being an academic theologian and social critic as was Niebuhr.[22]

There is more to this criticism of Niebuhr's, however. Graham himself has acknowledged the worthiness of some of this concern, and the years have shown him increasingly sensitive to and involved in other dimensions of Christian mission. The Billy Graham Evangelistic Association, for instance, has a fund that dispenses hundreds of thousands of dollars for disaster relief and development projects around the world. Graham's son and successor at the head of the BGEA, Franklin, has headed two organizations devoted especially to similar causes. More directly, Graham (ironically) has in fact been more involved in politics than Niebuhr in the 1950s could have guessed he would be—even as Graham has hardly shared Niebuhr's vision of what needed to be done in that arena! Politically a centrist figure in recent years, although he leaned toward the Republican Party in decades past, Graham cannot be faulted prima facie as uninterested in politics simply because he has not espoused the large-scale social engineering promoted by Niebuhr. In short, Graham

22. New York City pastor Henry P. Van Dusen did in fact make this point in a letter to Niebuhr's own journal, *Christianity and Crisis*. Indeed, he remarked that were it not for his initial conversion under the influence of Graham, he would not have gone on to explore the work of Niebuhr! See his letter, *Christianity and Crisis* 16 (2 April 1956): 40.

has not been dissociated from politics, nor has he avoided all social concerns. He has held, instead, to a much less interventionist political philosophy than Niebuhr's, and this principled position cannot be denounced merely as a lack of concern for the social and political per se. The point remains, though, that Graham concentrates on what he continues to believe is the only lasting solution to macro as well as micro problems: the one-by-one conversion of men and women to new life in Christ.

So what about the more popular version of this criticism, the revulsion toward emotion-laden, whip-'em-up revivals that vanish into the air, spiritually weightless and disconnected from the substantial presence of the local church? What about the related criticism that Graham seems to preach an instantaneous transformation of the soul with no regard for the continuing presence of temptations and sin in a person's life?

Graham crusades are held only with the prior commitment of a majority of local pastors and churches, so that the team from outside is as integrated as possible with the spiritual workers on site who will carry on afterward.[23] The extensive preparation carried out—sometimes a year or even two in advance—is not simply public relations. It also includes training volunteers, both lay and clerical, in evangelism and counseling and provides instruction in what is called "follow-up," the grounding of new believers in the basics of the faith and their integration into a church fellowship.

Then the crusade begins. After the mass choir and smooth soloist have sung, the greetings and testimonies from celebrities have been rendered, and Graham has stood up to preach, many observers have recorded their surprise at how unexpectedly mild are his sermons and particularly his invitation at the end to come forward to make a decision. He does and says virtually the same thing every time, and those who have endured the bombast of typical revivalist preaching in person or on television are pleasantly surprised at his moderation. Yet this tone is consistent with Graham's whole view: Only authentic decisions, only lasting commit-

23. On the importance of local effort, see Johnson, "Religious Crusade."

ments, are the goal; sheer emotional manipulation counts for nothing.

When one is ready to make such a spiritual decision at the meeting, no one has to walk forward and stand alone, even if one might think he or she is doing so! Counselor "captains" scan the audience for those who are responding to the invitation and then signal particular counselors—who are matched as closely as possible to the counsellee for sex, age, and so on—to walk forward with those particular persons and introduce themselves once in front of the platform. Graham remains briefly to instruct those who come forward at the end of the service, and then all adjourn to a counseling area for more conversation and teaching. Free literature is given to all who desire it, follow-up cards are filled out, and—usually overnight—the cards are processed and distributed to local pastors for contact.

The program of follow-up yet has weaknesses. Sometimes pastors fail to follow up properly; sometimes there is a poor match between inquirer and congregation; and so on. It is difficult to fault the Graham team and its sponsors, however, for not making considerable attempts to help those who make decisions at a service to find spiritual company in the weeks that follow. "One-shot" experiences clearly are not all they are after. (It is noteworthy in this regard that one-quarter of the first edition of *Peace with God* was devoted to follow-up, to going on in the Christian life. It dealt with topics ranging from personal piety, to morals, to church membership, to race and labor relations, and even contained a moral view of economics.)

The second set of criticisms—that the Graham efforts produce few genuine, deep, lasting conversions—also must be seen in the light of Graham's understanding of the Christian life and of conversion in particular. Of course, he might say, most people in the audience come from churches. Some are there bringing friends; others are there to be inspired; still others are there, even if they do not realize it themselves at first, to be themselves converted.[24] Most of America, after all, has been "churched" to some extent, but that says nothing about the genuineness of conversion experiences at this or that juncture.

24. McClelland and Hood, "In the Company of the Converted."

Furthermore, one does not always know when the decisive line has been crossed even for oneself. So while one might skip the "First Time Decision" box on the inquirer card and check instead "Rededication of Life," who is to say that this does not in fact mark the occasion of one's first authentic and lasting commitment to Christ and the actual regeneration of soul by the Holy Spirit?[25] Given Graham's own understanding of the Christian walk, the issue is absolutely moot. He and his team scrupulously avoid using the word *conversions* for what occurs at their meetings, preferring instead the more appropriately ambiguous term *decisions*.

Conclusions

When all is said and done in a Graham crusade—and a lot is said and done—the question of stewardship yet remains. Is the massive expenditure of time and money really worthwhile? The implication of Graham's conception of conversion is that answering this question is much more complicated than merely totting up numbers of previously unchurched people who make first-time professions of faith and go on to become regular church members, however much this is one target of the effort.

Indeed, the question of whether it is worthwhile is always a relative one: Is this the best means relative to the others available to a given community of Christians? Graham would never argue, and has never argued, that so-called mass evangelism should ever displace local evangelism. Indeed, the popular Billy Graham Schools (seminars) of Evangelism have been set up across the continent precisely to foster local, small-scale evangelism. But can mass evangelism of this sort play an important part, as a kind of "crisis" event itself in the midst of the "process" of local mission?

Of course, the very fact of mixed results, of less-than-overwhelming numerical success, does not immediately daunt

25. Graham himself later testified that he checked "Recommitment" on the card he filled out as a teenager at Ham's meetings, even though he believes that episode was his decisive conversion experience (*Just As I Am*, 30).

Christians who follow, after all, a preacher who himself told a parable of an only "partly" successful sower of seed. Indeed, this itinerant rabbi's preaching was itself not universally popular. Assessing Graham's crusades remains withal a difficult question to answer in terms of social science, in terms of observable, quantifiable data, precisely because of the nature of the question, among other reasons. How in fact does one measure the success of a Graham crusade given its diffuse concern to revitalize churches and bring people to fresh commitments to Christ?

To do so, one must maintain clear definitions of key terms such as *conversion, alternation,* and *commitment.*[26]

Conversion, according to sociologists Irwin Barker and Raymond Currie, "is defined as a radical break with one's former identity such that the past and the present are antithetical in some important respects." *Alternation* is "a transition in which a new identity develops naturally out of the old one. Unlike a conversion, the old identity is not radically disrupted; minor, rather than fundamental changes are experienced."[27] And *commitment* is measured by the intellectual, experiential, and practical ways in which one's "adhesion" to the new identity manifests itself.

Given his theological understanding of conversion as an act of God in the human soul, Graham sees the above-mentioned definitions of *conversion* or *alternation* as describing a genuine spiritual death-to-life transition in a person's life and thus a genuine conversion. Yet however much one's outward life patterns might change (at least briefly) in the case of conversion, there might still be no actual conversion of the soul. On the other hand, however little one's outward life patterns might change in the case of alternation, a genuine conversion, according to Graham, might still have taken place and thus is nonetheless as radical a change as can be imag-

26. See R. V. Travisano, "Alternation and Conversion as Qualitatively Different Transformations," in *Social Psychology through Symbolic Interaction,* ed. G. P. Stone and H. A. Farberman (Waltham, Mass.: Ginn-Blaisdell, 1970), 594–606. Cf. the similar distinction between *conversion* and *adhesion* in A. D. Nock, *Conversion* (New York: Oxford University Press, 1933); and William C. Shepherd, "Conversion and Adhesion," *Sociological Inquiry* 49 (1979): 251–63.

27. Barker and Currie, "Converts," 305.

ined. Whenever there has been a genuine conversion, however, Graham clearly expects to see increased commitment or adhesion.

It may be, then, that social scientists will continue to be fascinated by the "radical" conversion paradigm and will indeed find instances of such at a Graham crusade. But they will also find, according to Graham, a broad spectrum of genuine conversions (that is, spiritual *changes*) as well, none of which ought to be literally discounted as conversions simply because the people show a less obvious change of life pattern.[28]

The assessment of Graham crusades in terms of conversions—an endeavor pursued equally by both sociologists and Graham's own evangelical supporters—therefore, can be either artificially constricted (only the radical conversions of current sociological parlance will be counted) or actually hopeless (who can say who is actually converted in Graham's theological sense of the term?). While social science cannot expect to gauge the latter (which is, after all, the province of the last judgment), it perhaps ought not to persist in the former.

Instead, one might well attempt an assessment in line with the claimed purposes and results of such crusades.[29] In a longitudinal study over at least five or ten years, evidence can be adduced regarding the following indications of commitment or adhesion: church attendance, involvement in other church and parachurch activities (e.g., tithing and volunteer work), Christian marriage and other key associations, child rearing according to ostensibly Christian principles, and so on. Moreover, since in this construal any individual case is ultimately mysterious (since some "fall away" or—in another Protestant theological construction—they were never "soundly converted"

28. So Snow and Machalek: "It is not entirely clear . . . where conversion begins and ends. . . . In fact, it is not evident that only the more radical type of change should be conceptualized as conversion" ("Sociology of Conversion," 170).

29. So Lewis R. Rambo, "Conversion: Toward a Holistic Model of Religious Change," *Pastoral Psychology* 38 (1989): 47–48; and Scott Thumma, "Seeking to Be Converted: An Examination of Recent Conversion Studies and Theories," *Pastoral Psychology* 39 (1991): 191–92.

in the first place), similar questions ought to be asked of participating church groups regarding increased attendance and activity, more vital *esprit de corps*, more candidates for professional pastoral ministry, and so on. (Indeed, it is precisely in these terms, rather than in terms of sheer numbers of conversions, that some of Graham's own apologists vouch for the worthiness of the massive crusade efforts.)[30]

Finally, Lewis Rambo suggests that "genuine" conversion is defined and elicited by a particular group's set of normative prescriptions and proscriptions. The scholarly enterprise, therefore, should be descriptive rather than normative. Scholars should observe, understand, interpret, and explain conversion as it is actually advocated and practiced.[31] Social scientists, therefore, might well formulate their inquiries regarding conversion and commitment on the basis of preliminary inquiries of the individuals and groups themselves: "You say you have experienced conversion. What does this mean and how is it evidenced?" The present study suggests something of the importance of this approach.

As in any quest to reduce chaos to order and then complexity to simplicity, social scientists risk reductionism, coercing data to fit into their paradigms. However frustrating it may be for a social scientific interpreter looking on from the outside, therefore, Graham's paradigm of conversion cautions one against using Graham crusade conversion experiences as paradigm cases of single-moment conversions, since crusade decisions are in fact so varied. Moreover, Graham's conception of conversion as having multiple possible trajectories cautions social scientists against relying on simplistic paradigms of conversion simply because they make (artificially) easier the task of totting up and sorting out conversion experiences for social scientific study. It will not do for social scientists to say that some kinds of conversions just "don't count."

---

30. The oeuvre of John Pollock is an accessible, clear example: *Billy Graham: The Authorized Biography* (New York: McGraw-Hill, 1966); *Billy Graham: Evangelist to the World* (New York: Harper & Row, 1978); *To All the Nations: The Billy Graham Story* (San Francisco: Harper & Row, 1985).

31. Rambo, "Conversion," 48.

8

Women in Public Ministry

Five Models in Twentieth-Century
North American Evangelicalism

— Ignorance of bible is interpreted

The panel of distinguished denominational leaders sat on the conference stage. "The next question for the panel is this," said the moderator. "Should women be allowed to preach in church?"

The moderator turned to his right and acknowledged one of the elder statesmen of the denomination. "Yes, Dr. Doulton?"

The tall, thin, bespectacled man leaned into the microphone. The crowd hushed as it prepared to listen to a disquisition on this complicated subject. "The Bible says women should keep silent in church," he snapped. "That's good enough for me!"[1]

For many Canadian and American evangelicals,[2] this answer to a theological and practical problem would have been correct

---

1. I was witness to this exchange at a conference in 1975, disguised here only slightly.

2. *Evangelical* is used here in a broad sense, denoting not only those who currently use the name to describe themselves, the so-called neo-evangelicals, but also all those who maintain the traditional evangelical emphases on the unique authority of Scripture, the necessity of a vital personal faith, and the importance of evangelism. Thus, what is said here, although drawn mostly from firsthand research in white Canadian and northern American sources, I suggest is largely true for black and southern evangelicals as well. On this and other uses of *evangelical* in the American context, see George M. Marsden, "The Evangelical Denomination," in *Evangelicalism and Modern America*, ed. George M. Marsden (Grand Rapids: Eerdmans, 1984), vii–xvi. For discussion of evangelicalism in Canada, see John G. Stackhouse, Jr., *Canadian Evangelicalism in the Twentieth Century: An Introduction to Its Character* (Toronto: University of Toronto Press, 1993).

in all three of its parts: immediate reference to the Bible ("The Bible says . . ."); satisfaction with the literal exegesis that the Bible in fact does say, "women should keep silent in church"; and contentment with a straightforward application of this un- ambiguous proof-text without need of further consideration ("That's good enough for me!").

Other evangelicals, however—including those with exactly the same commitment to biblical authority, literal exegesis, and straightforward application—have seen the issue differently. These Christians, especially those in Holiness or Pentecostal traditions but also those within a variety of other communions, have held that the Bible (and especially the New Testament) teaches the essential and functional equality of men and women in the church.[3]

3. The number of women in evangelical leadership, however, even includ- ing Pentecostal leaders, has been very small, especially since the middle of the twentieth century (Margaret L. Bendroth, "The Search for 'Women's Role' in American Evangelicalism, 1930–1980," in *Evangelicalism and Modern America*, 123). An important monograph on this subject demonstrating that more evan- gelicals believed in this pattern earlier in this century is Janette Hassey, *No Time for Silence: Evangelical Women in Public Ministry around the Turn of the Century* (Grand Rapids: Zondervan, 1986); see also Margaret L. Bendroth, "Fundamentalism and Feminity: The Reorientation of Women's Role in the 1920s," *Evangelical Studies Bulletin* 5 (March 1988): 1–4. A broad historical sketch of women in public ministry has been provided in Ruth A. Tucker and Walter Liefeld, *Daughters of the Church: Women and Ministry from New Testa- ment Times to the Present* (Grand Rapids: Zondervan, 1987). For Tucker's own reflections on these issues, see Ruth A. Tucker, *Women in the Maze: Questions and Answers on Biblical Equality* (Downers Grove, Ill.: InterVarsity, 1992). See also Lynda L. Coon, Katherine J. Haldane, and Elisabeth W. Sommer, eds., *That Gentle Strength: Historical Perspectives on Women in Christianity* (Charlottes- ville, Va.: University Press of Virginia, 1990). And for an even broader context, see Denise Lardner Carmody, *Women and World Religions*, 2d ed. (1979; re- print, Englewood Cliffs, N.J.: Prentice Hall, 1989).

The roots of this debate among Canadian and especially American evangel- icals go back to the early nineteenth century. See, for example, Carroll Smith- Rosenberg, "Women and Religious Revivals: Anti-Ritualism, Liminality, and the Emergence of the American Bourgeoisie," and Nancy A. Hewitt, "The Pe- rimeters of Women's Power in American Religion," in *The Evangelical Tradi- tion in America*, ed. Leonard I. Sweet (Macon, Ga.: Mercer University Press, 1984), 199–231 and 233–56. Sweet's bibliographical essay, which introduces this work, points the way to a number of other sources on this subject. See "The Evangelical Tradition in America," 56–67. For other nineteenth-century bibliography, see Edith L. Blumhofer, "Evangelical Ministering Women," *Evan- gelical Studies Bulletin* 5 (March 1988): 6–9.

Both persons within North American evangelicalism and observers outside it have tended to characterize the evangelical
debate over this issue in terms of these virtual polar opposites.[4]
It is perhaps easier to argue for one position over the other
when the debate is cast in these terms.[5] But if one takes into account not only churches but also a broad range of evangelical
organizations, one observes that rather than two options, evangelicals in fact have chosen from among at least five different
models for understanding the opportunities for women in public ministry. Examination of these five models will show, furthermore, that evangelicals have developed and worked within
these models while maintaining their characteristic commitments to the fundamental authority of Scripture in faith and
practice, to literal exegesis, and to direct application of scriptural principles and practices to modern life.[6]

Model 1: The Silent, Submissive Majority

The model for women in public ministry among Canadian
and American evangelicals that has been most commonly articulated in our time is that women have virtually no public ministry in terms of exercising authority or verbally participating in
the meetings of the church—that is, of the entire congregation.

An apparent exception often seen within the terms of this
model merely proves the rule: Women often have taught males
in mixed Sunday school classes, but only until the boys reached
an age determined as being "too old" (that is, too close to manhood) to sit under a woman's teaching. Then they had to be
taught by men.

4. So also says Bendroth, "Search for 'Women's Role,'" 122–23, 134.
5. For two of many examples, see W. Ward Gasque, "The Role of Women in
the Church, in Society, and in the Home," *Crux* 19 (September 1983): 3–9; and
David Basinger, "Gender Roles, Scripture, and Science: Some Clarifications,"
Christian Scholar's Review 17 (March 1988): 241–53.
6. For a discussion of especially the first two of these three aspects of the
view of the Bible among American (and also, I suggest, among Canadian) evangelicals, see Mark A. Noll, *Between Faith and Criticism: Evangelicals, Scholarship, and the Bible in America* (San Francisco: Harper & Row, 1986), especially
142–61.

Women also may have been involved in ministries to children or other women, but not to men and not in the context of the full church. In the view of these evangelicals, this practice depends on such biblical teaching as the following: "Christ is the head of every man, and the man is the head of a woman" (1 Cor. 11:3 NASB); "the women [must] keep silent in the churches; for they are not permitted to speak, but are to subject themselves. . . . For it is improper for a woman to speak in church" (1 Cor. 14:34–35 NASB); and "Let a woman quietly receive instruction with entire submissiveness. But I do not allow a woman to teach or exercise authority over a man, but to remain quiet" (1 Tim. 2:11–12 NASB).[7]

Therefore, following this model, evangelical women—who have constituted the majority of the members of most evangelical churches (as they have most churches everywhere)—have not preached, taught, or exercised pastoral leadership in their churches. While serving eminently in most other areas of church life, when leadership of the whole church per se is at issue, they have formed a conspicuously invisible majority.

Certain common practices among such evangelical churches, however, show that this model has been under considerable strain. For instance, almost none of these churches has forbidden women from participating in congregational singing. Furthermore, women frequently have sung solos from the pulpit or platform of the church, leading some to wonder if they would have been allowed to preach de facto if only they would have set their sermons to music. The logic that a woman should not conduct the service, lead the singing, and so on, since this would be "exercising authority," should also have forbidden a woman from clearly directing the worship through song. And so, in the same way, the apostle's apparent

7. This is not to gainsay the common charge of sexism leveled at those who hold this or any of the other models short of model 5. It is, however, to recognize the legitimate problems evangelicals face in dealing with the scriptural teachings regarding this issue and therefore to attribute good faith at least to the many evangelicals who manifest no sexist attitudes in other parts of life and yet feel bound by interpretations of Scripture that lead to options other than model 5. See, for example, Bruce Waltke, "The Relationship of the Sexes in the Bible," *Crux* 19 (September 1983): 10–16.

silencing of women should have forbidden public singing of any kind.[8]

Many evangelicals of this sort have also read books and listened to tapes by women authors or speakers that clearly offer opinions on matters of biblical interpretation and theology. Many of them have also enjoyed small group meetings or even public services in which women have "shared" testimonies of spiritual experience that often have included remarks on the Bible.[9] On a different level, women have made their opinions known in many churches by voting—even, indeed, by voting on who will lead the churches as pastors, deacons, and so on—as members of churches that have congregational polities.[10]

Clearly, model 1, therefore, which is so apparently austere and simple, has been stretched and complicated in practice. The "silent, submissive majority" has made what contributions it could therein, even as each new generation of church leaders has struggled to implement the "clear teachings of Scripture" in the context of manifest, if almost universally appreciated, inconsistencies.

Model 5: Equal Partners in Ministry

At the other end of the spectrum (hence the numbering scheme of this chapter) lies the view that gender makes no difference in the church. God gifts people for public ministry without regard to sex, and God did so throughout the history of the

8. An allowance is made by evangelical seminary professor Wayne Grudem for women prophesying in church, but not teaching, since he sees the latter ministry carrying authority in the New Testament in a way the former does not. This is an allowance, however, rendered less impressive than it might first appear by the fact that few evangelical churches besides the Pentecostal or charismatic churches make room for the exercise of the gift of prophecy—whether exercised by men or women. See Wayne Grudem, "Prophecy—Yes, but Teaching—No: Paul's Consistent Advocacy of Women's Participation without Governing Authority," *Journal of the Evangelical Theological Society* 30 (March 1987): 11–23.

9. These observations come from Walter L. Liefeld, "Women and the Nature of Ministry," *Journal of the Evangelical Theological Society* 30 (March 1987): 49.

10. For this point, as for several others, I am indebted to a letter received from Janette Hassey that commented on an earlier draft of this paper (letter to author, 16 September 1987).

church—even in New Testament times. Indeed (and for some this is the crucial argument), in these "last days" God has poured out his Spirit among people of all sorts—including both men and women—to extend the gospel message.

While shared by increasing numbers of evangelicals of various stripes, this model has been most prevalent in the Holiness-Pentecostal wing of evangelicalism. The most notable denominational example of this model in both countries is perhaps the Salvation Army, which, from the earliest powerful influence of Catherine Booth on both her husband and the denomination itself, has promoted egalitarian public ministry.[11] The most notable individual example in both Canada and the United States is perhaps Aimee Semple McPherson (1890–1944), whose flamboyant career in Southern California as founder of the International Church of the Foursquare Gospel has obscured for many her origins and early ministry in Canada. Many Canadian Pentecostals, however, know that "Sister Aimee" led important and popular revival services in a number of Canadian centers before establishing her base in the United States.[12]

Evangelicals have supported this model because they believe the Bible says that God created men and women in his image and as coequal rulers of the world. The latter relationship changed only with the curse of Genesis 3. The Bible also says that "all of you . . . were baptized into Christ. . . . There is neither . . . male nor female, for you are all one in Christ Jesus" (Gal. 3:27–28). The descriptions of spiritual gifts in the Pauline corpus nowhere link gifts of teaching or other leadership to men (see, for example, 1 Corinthians 12, 14; Eph. 4:7–16), and women in the New Testament apparently exercised teaching

11. See R. G. Moyles, *The Blood and Fire in Canada: A History of the Salvation Army in the Dominion 1882–1976* (Toronto: Peter Martin Associates, 1977); E. H. McKinley, *Marching to Glory: The History of the Salvation Army in the United States 1880–1980* (San Francisco: Harper & Row, 1980); and Donald W. Dayton, *Discovering an Evangelical Heritage* (New York: Harper & Row, 1976), 94–95.

12. On Aimee Semple McPherson, see, among many other works, Alvyn Austin, *Aimee Semple McPherson* (Don Mills, Ontario: Fitzhenry and Whiteside, 1980); Edith L. Blumhofer, *Aimee Semple McPherson: Everybody's Sister* (Grand Rapids: Eerdmans, 1993); and William G. McLoughlin, "Aimee Semple McPherson: 'Your Sister in the King's Glad Service,'" *Journal of Popular Culture* 1 (winter 1967): 193–217.

and leading ministries (e.g., the teaching of Priscilla in Acts 18:26; the description of Phoebe as a deacon and of Junia as an apostle in Rom. 16:1, 7). All of this is consonant with the prophecy cited by Peter on the first post-ascension Pentecost that God promised to pour out his spirit on men and women in the "last days," which days have manifestly come (Acts 2:17–18; cf. Joel 2:28–29). Therefore, according to this model, evangelical women who have demonstrated that God gifted and called them to exercise gifts in public ministry have been free to do so.

For every Aimee Semple McPherson in this century, however, there have been, well, virtually all the rest of the high-profile preachers. Roberta Hestenes has emerged as an American role model in recent decades, as Eastern College president and then senior pastor of a large American congregation. Maxine Hancock, on the Canadian side of the border, has moved from a ministry aimed at women to speaking, writing, and broadcasting to a wide audience both within and outside the church. Very few other women, however, have taken a place among the leaders of these traditions. Even among Christians who teach this pattern, women have yet to attain numbers in leadership in proportion to their numbers in the pews.

The Confrontation between Models 1 and 5

Lest the impression be left that those who have thought in terms of the two models described merely have selected the texts that have suited them and ignored the others, it should be noted that each group has dealt with at least some of the other's favorite texts and interpreted them according to its own understanding. Model 1 ("The Silent, Submissive Majority"), for instance, typically has understood Galatians 3:28 as applying to equality in the reception of spiritual salvation, not to the eradication of temporary social roles. It has dismissed the lack of sexual specificity regarding the gifts in some passages on the grounds that these passages are supplemented by other texts that limit certain roles (and thus gifts) to men. It has interpreted the few instances of female leadership in the New Testament in ways that have preserved the basic pattern: Thus, Priscilla taught Apollos in concert with (and presumably submission to) her husband, Aquila, and only in her home, not in the church; and "Junia" is probably a textual corruption of the masculine "Junias." It has understood Acts 2 to speak indeed of a general outpouring of God's spirit for world evangelization, but with the qualification that women are not to preach publicly but rather to witness privately.

For its part, model 5 ("Equal Partners in Ministry") typically has characterized the passages forbidding women's teaching or exercising authority as applying directly only to the situation addressed (for example, noisy, ignorant women in Corinth or Ephesus). The basic principle shines above and even through these passages that women, once properly educated and supported by the church, can take their rightful places alongside men in each ministry of the church.

Thus, both sides have deflected the other's charges, interpreting "problematic" texts in the light of "clear" ones, both remaining faithful to the authority of the Bible, literal exegesis, and direct application.[13]

Model 2: The Missionary Exception

Among those evangelicals who have ostensibly subscribed to model 1, there have been some who have supported an even more significant exception that decidedly has not proven the

13. The literature on this question is immense, but for an unusually thorough and well-balanced presentation of both models 1 and 5, see Robert K. Johnson, "The Role of Women in the Church and Home: An Evangelical Testcase in Hermeneutics," in *Scripture, Tradition, and Interpretation: Essays Presented to Everett F. Harrison by His Students and Colleagues in Honor of His Seventy-Fifth Birthday*, ed. W. Ward Gasque and William Sanford LaSor (Grand Rapids: Eerdmans, 1978), 234–59.

Variations of biblical interpretation within these two models are charted by Jack Buckley in "Paul, Women, and the Church: How Fifteen Modern Interpreters Understand Five Key Passages," *Eternity* 31 (December 1980): 30–35. Tucker and Liefeld (in *Daughters of the Church*) provide a bibliographical essay and also a discussion of many of the central theological and exegetical issues at stake: for the former, see 401–34; for the latter, see 435–71. They also provide a bibliography (511–40), as does Gilbert Bilezikian in his *Beyond Sex Roles: A Guide for the Study of Female Roles in the Bible* (Grand Rapids: Baker, 1985), 269–91. A more recent bibliography can be found in Mary Stewart Van Leeuwen, ed., *After Eden: Facing the Challenge of Gender Reconciliation* (Grand Rapids: Eerdmans; Carlisle: Paternoster, 1993), 601–46.

rule. This is the exception made for female missionaries, especially for those going to Third World, "pagan" countries. In this situation, women have exercised all the teaching and leadership gifts they have been able to draw upon as they have pioneered Christianity in the most inhospitable places. Women have evangelized and discipled entire villages and regions. With this success, many women naturally have gone on to preside over the establishment of churches and the training of leaders.

Up to this point, at least, the evangelicals who have practiced model 2 have done so with the following understanding: (1) Women in this case are not leading a church per se because one is just being founded, and thus the situation does not fall under the biblical prescriptions against church leadership; and (2) once a church has been founded and is well established under indigenous, male leadership (a process that, admittedly, can take some years, during which time the female missionary functions in fact as a pastor), the woman is obliged to withdraw from all public ministry therein. One leader among the Christian (or Plymouth) Brethren, a small denomination well respected for its proportionately large contribution to foreign missions, speaks for many evangelicals:

> When, after much patient labor, souls have been won for Christ, and indigenous converts have learned the pattern of New Testament church gathering, many of these godly pioneer sisters have kept loyal faith with the principles [regarding the subordination of women in the church] described above, and have rejoiced to sit in "quietness" while men, raised up of God from what had been "raw" heathenism, ministered the Word and led in praise and prayer in the local church gatherings.[14]

These evangelicals have often recognized, however, that the first point here is considerably stronger than the second point. The second point still allows a woman to teach men and to exercise authority over men, sometimes for years.

This apparent inconsistency generally has been justified by recourse to what might be called the "missionary exception." That

---

14. G. Fred Hamilton, *Why? Why Practice New Testament Principles Today?* (Spring Lake, N.J.: Christian Missions in Many Lands, 1985), 58–59. Not all Brethren, to be sure, would endorse this view: Some would observe model 1 more strictly; others would support others of the models, including model 5.

is, the need for evangelism is so great that if men won't pursue it, women should. God, after all, has often brought good out of what normally would have been regarded as evil (e.g., Joseph sold into slavery as the beginning of a chain of events that would lead to the salvation of Egypt and Israel).[15] This point usually has been followed, not by a rethinking of whether women should be allowed to teach or exercise authority at home ("Well, if we let them minister on the mission field, and they are undoubtedly effective, why not let them minister here?"), but by a scolding of the men in the audience for not taking up their rightful part in the missionary enterprise, a part that would presumably render women's public ministry superfluous.

In some cases this attitude might indicate an implicit (or not-so-implicit) racism: It's okay for the natives but not for us.[16] But usually it indicates simply the evangelical commitment to evangelism, a commitment that has overridden and therefore modified the otherwise "clear" teaching about public ministry.

The biblical justification for this position (justification that is necessary, it should be remembered, for all evangelicals) usually has been given in the deductive mode just presented. Given the commitment to the principle of evangelism, as taught by the Bible, then it follows that . . . and so on. Some evangelicals, to be sure, have had recourse to the explicit (that is, proof-text) type of biblical justification, using passages referring to the Great Commission that encourage Christians (apparently without gender limitation) to "make disciples, baptizing . . . and teaching," or Acts 2, which talks about God pouring out his spirit on men and women in the last days. But texts such as Matthew 28 and Acts 2, to other readers, go farther than the evangelicals who have elected this option would want to go, since they seem to have obvious implications for women in all sorts of public ministry. The deductive method, therefore, has worked better for this model than proof-texting, and the evangelical penchant for citing specific texts has been honored often simply by biblical illustrations rather than instructions.

15. The latter point comes from the Hassey letter.

16. Tucker and Liefeld recognize this as well: "Some would-be critics took comfort in the fact that most women missionaries . . . who were preaching to mixed or all-male groups were not seriously breaching any Pauline injunctions anyway, since their hearers were only 'natives'" (*Daughters of the Church*, 291).

The following example is taken from the writings of L. E. Maxwell, founder of the Prairie Bible Institute in Alberta, one of the leading training centers of evangelical missionaries in this century:

> When so many ministers of the stronger and wiser sex are useless or worse than useless in the work of soul saving, and preach for years without being instrumental in a single conversion, is there not a cause for woman's ministry? . . . [Yet] had Barak better played the man, Deborah had better played the woman. . . . Had the disciples tarried longer at the sepulchre, Mary need not have been the first proclaimer of our Lord.[17]

Deb.

This paragraph demonstrates the essential tension in this model between a basic commitment to male leadership and an even more basic commitment to effective evangelization. This tension is relaxed only when the church founded by the missionary is capable of self-leadership and therefore no longer in need of the missionary's leadership.[18]

Model 3: The Parachurch Parenthesis

Many evangelicals who would not have thought of having women teach or lead in churches have sent millions of dollars, not to mention their sons and daughters, to the wide range of evangel-

17. L. E. Maxwell, "'The Weaker Sex,'" *Prairie Overcomer* 39 (April 1966): 130. (The *Prairie Overcomer* and the *Prairie Pastor*, noted below, were published by the Prairie Bible Institute, Three Hills, Alberta.)
Dorothy Pape quotes noted dispensational scholar Charles C. Ryrie making the same point: "We need to remember Paul not only commanded that things be done decently and in order but also that they be done. In such cases [that is, foreign mission fields on which no man will serve] . . . it is better to do the work with qualified women—even though this is not ideal—than to sit back and do nothing because there are no men. However, women must be cautioned against continuing such work after there are men available" (*The Place of Women in the Church* [Chicago: Moody, 1968], n.p.; quoted in Dorothy Pape, *In Search of God's Ideal Woman: A Personal Examination of the New Testament* [Downers Grove, Ill.: InterVarsity, 1976], 246).
18. And this tension, by the way, would tempt the leaders of the sending church to recognize such a state before it existed in order to "call off" the woman missionary.

ical parachurch groups that have sprung up in Canada and the United States, especially since World War II. In many of these parachurch groups, however, women have often exercised the same functions as men: They have taught the Scriptures, presided over worship services, provided spiritual counsel, and sat on the executive boards of local chapters and national organizations.[19]

InterVarsity Christian Fellowship (IVCF), one of the best-established of these groups in both countries, throughout its history has welcomed women onto its staff. Indeed, several decades ago the Canadian organization appointed a woman to the office of divisional director (roughly equivalent to a vice presidency) without apparent backlash from the constituency.

The reason this community could support such ministry by women was articulated briefly but decisively by C. Stacey Woods, pioneer of IVCF in Canada and the United States: "Inter-Varsity is not a church, it is a free fellowship of Christian students meeting in the name of the Lord Jesus Christ to witness to their student friends regarding the saving grace of Jesus Christ."[20] That is, since InterVarsity is basically an evangelistic organization, not a church, the biblical teachings about the subordination of women in the church do not apply. Evangelicals can support IVCF and a variety of other organizations that allow women to exercise gifts not recognized as such within the local church or denomination because these groups are, in this sense, not part of the church as the Bible describes it.

The fact that almost none within this wide range of parachurch groups has ever named a woman to its highest office, however, leads one to wonder if yet another model has been applied, model 4.

19. For a sketch of women involved with such ministries, see Tucker and Liefeld, *Daughters of the Church*, 392–99. Janette Hassey remarks, however, that other evangelical parachurch groups (she mentions Campus Crusade for Christ) do limit the ministry of women, usually along the lines of model 1 (letter).

20. C. Stacey Woods, *The Growth of a Work of God: The Story of the Early Days of the Inter-Varsity Christian Fellowship of the United States of America as Told by Its First General Secretary* (Downers Grove, Ill.: InterVarsity, 1978), 118. For more on IVCF in the United States, see Keith and Gladys Hunt, *For Christ and the University: The Story of InterVarsity Christian Fellowship of the U.S.A., 1940–1990* (Downers Grove, Ill.: InterVarsity, 1991).

Model 4: The "Under Authority" Arrangement

In this scheme, women can exercise public gifts of teaching and preaching, whether in churches, Bible schools, parachurch groups, and so on, as long as they are "under the authority" of male leadership.[21]

The concern here has been to honor such biblical passages as 1 Corinthians 11:3; Ephesians 5:22–24; and 1 Timothy 2:12, which have been understood as forbidding a Christian woman to exercise authority over a Christian man, and in particular forbidding a Christian wife to exercise authority over her Christian husband. The "anti-teaching" passages, however, have been seen to be of "local application," that is, applying only to the specific instance Paul was addressing in his epistles.

D. R. Miller, a graduate of New York and Columbia Universities who taught in American and Canadian Bible schools during the first half of this century, set out this position in a statement titled "On Women Speaking." In discussing 1 Corinthians 14, for instance, she declares that

> the salient point here is the "being in obedience." This goes right back to Gen. 3:16. The Law does not say keep silence, it says "be in obedience." . . .
>
> Now, if we accept from our hearts this decree of God vesting headship in the man, then other things fall into order. There will be no "usurping of authority," no "teaching" in the way of laying down the law to a man, no assertion of the right to teach. All will be under authority.[22]

Miller goes on to recite several of the biblical passages detailed above under model 5 ("Equal Partners in Ministry"), but then concludes with this application:

21. Hassey points out that this authority is understood by congregationalist groups to reside in the congregration itself, so some say that women can preach and so on as long as the congregation agrees (letter). This again demonstrates the exception noted above in the discussion of model 1: The "invisible majority" can exercise authority de facto and even, indeed, de jure through congregational voting.

22. D. R. Miller, "On Women Speaking," *Prairie Pastor* 12 (December 1939): 8.

If your husband thinks you should not bring the message when he is away, then as a Christian wife you should not do it. If the elders of your church object to your doing so, then you should keep silence gladly. But if they feel that you have a gift that God can use as a blessing in their church, then, I should say have one of them lead the service and you give the message. Let a man be very evidently at the head. Let it be evident that you are in subjection and that the very fact of your giving the message springs from your subjection to man's headship.[23]

R. Pierce Beaver has noted that this model dominated the involvement of women in nineteenth-century American missions. Married women under the authority of their husbands were much more welcome to serve than were single women.[24] In our own time, evangelicals prominent in Canada and the United States and as diverse as theologian J. I. Packer and faith healer Kathryn Kuhlman have defended women's public ministry as long as it is exercised under the authority of male leaders.[25]

Following this model, then, women have been free to fill any office of the church except the highest, whether deacon (in certain churches this is not the highest and so is open to women), elder, pastor, or priest. They have preached, but only under the authority of male authorities—ecclesiastical always, and marital where applicable.

Given that much of the Scripture understood under model 1 as universally applicable is understood here as culture-bound and occasion-specific, however, some evangelicals might well wonder if it is such a large step from model 4 to model 5.

23. Ibid.
24. See R. Pierce Beaver, *American Protestant Women in World Mission: A History of the First Feminist Movement in North America*, rev. ed. (Grand Rapids: Eerdmans, 1980), 35. This pattern continues to characterize many evangelical missions.
25. For Packer, see Robert K. Johnston, "Biblical Authority and Interpretation: The Test Case of Women's Role in the Church and Home Updated," in *Women, Authority, and the Bible*, ed. Alvera Mickelsen (Downers Grove, Ill.: InterVarsity, 1986), 38–39; for Kuhlman, see Tucker and Liefeld, *Daughters of the Church*, 392–94. This also seems to be the line of application for John Nolland's study, "Women in the Public Life of the Church," *Crux* 19 (September 1983): 17–23.

Conclusion

This survey of different evangelical models of female public ministry leads to several observations. First, the traditional evangelical polemic that the "other" side in the debate is not true to the biblical text falls down on two counts. In the first place, there is not just one "other side" but a variety of options that need consideration. In the second place, each of the options can be seen fairly as holding to a traditional regard for the unique authority of Scripture, literal exegesis, and straightforward application of text to faith and practice. The debate then is over what is the best interpretation and application of the relevant texts, not over these first principles.[26]

Second, the first four models are not discrete types. Models 2 ("The Missionary Exception") and 3 ("The Parachurch Parenthesis") are clearly compatible with each other and are each a variation on model 1 ("The Silent, Submissive Majority"). Further, arguments for the public ministry of women have often drawn on the arguments of more than one of the middle three options, depending on the issue at hand.[27]

Third, despite the widely held view that evangelicals have practiced either model 1 (complete silence) or model 5 (full participation), relatively few in fact have practiced either extreme consistently. The dominant pattern has been an articulation of the principles of model 1 with the practice of one or more of models 2, 3, and 4.

26. For an underscoring of this point and a recent sampling of this debate, see the essays and responses in Mickelsen, *Women, Authority, and the Bible.*

A different debate among Christians identified with evangelicalism, however, is between proponents of one or more of the models described above and those who argue that the apostle Paul was either unhelpfully culturally conditioned in his views of or just plain wrong about women's roles, and therefore, much of his teaching on this subject is not authoritative (for examples, see the work of Paul King Jewett and Virginia Ramey Mollenkott noted in the bibliographies cited above).

This last model, therefore, has the same conclusion as model 5 ("Equal Partners in Ministry") but differs importantly from the other five options in its basic understanding of Scripture and theology and therefore is not included in this typology. (Grant Wacker pointed out this sixth model in a letter commenting on an earlier draft of this paper.)

27. See, for example, L. E. Maxwell's defense of Miller appended to her "On Women Speaking," 8.

Fourth, models 1 to 4, which restrict the public ministry of women to at least some extent, have come under strain from three powerful forces within. The first is the evident worthiness of at least some types of public ministry performed by women, ministry that cannot be simply discounted. Whether it be Sunday school teaching and singing in model 1, or teaching and exercising authority in other contexts in the other three, each model can be seen as carrying the seeds of its own supplanting. Indeed, both L. E. Maxwell and D. R. Miller serve as illustrations yet again in that both use arguments from experience to justify their positions as much as arguments from Scripture—even as, to be sure, their status as evangelicals requires that they ultimately must see agreement between the Spirit's subjective witness and his testimony in the Bible. Maxwell writes, just before the paragraph in which he defends his position from Scripture, that

> according to certain legalistic positions held in the present day, Miss Miller has been out of order all of these past years when she has been so blessedly used of God in the training of hundreds of young people. While certain persons might contentiously hold for technicalities of the letter, God's Spirit, the Spirit which gives liberty and not bondage, uses yielded men and women to further his glory.[28]

Miller herself indicates that during at least some of her time of public ministry "I had been led at each step not so much by the teaching of Scripture as by the still small voice of the Spirit,"[29] even as she goes on to defend her position with exegesis in the paragraphs that follow.

As noted in discussing model 2 ("The Missionary Exception"), however, evangelical adherence to the "plain teaching of Scripture" often has weathered the storm even of what to some is strong experiential evidence for the legitimacy of women's public ministry. Many evangelicals simply have admitted that God has blessed certain women in unusual situations and that he, as one woman writes, "is willing to use us in spite of our imperfections"—that is, in spite of our employing women in such

28. Ibid.
29. Ibid, 7. The same testimony is given a generation later by Dorothy Pape, a career missionary in Japan. See Pape, *In Search of God's Ideal Woman*, 153–55.

roles and thus contravening the scriptural pattern of leadership.[30] These evangelicals, therefore, have maintained a pattern of scriptural interpretation and interpreted this experience of women's ministry through it—however plausible or implausible this construing of that experience might seem to others.

We here note, then, simply that the experience of women exercising gifts of public ministry, coupled with the conviction that the Spirit's subjective testimony never contradicts his testimony in the Bible, has provoked two kinds of responses among evangelicals. One response has been a new interpretation of Scripture that squares with this experience.[31] The other has been what some would see as a downplaying or belittling of this ministry in the interest of squaring it with a traditional interpretation of Scripture.

The second force that has compelled evangelicals at least to modify their employment of women in public ministry has come from the opposite direction. Young women raised in the church or adult converts who have come into it have seen, in at least some extreme versions of model 1, the stultifying of the older women in the church who have kept or been kept very silent. These women have never expressed an opinion in a church meeting, have never led the congregation in prayer, have never taught other adults something they learned in their private Bible study.[32] Many of the other women in the church who have seen the evident results of this extreme version of the model—the apparent inability of many of these women to form an opinion about any important subject without their husbands' guidance; their inability to speak plainly and directly about a problem and their tendency to resort to thin humor or third parties to express disagreement, even with other

30. Gertrud Harlow, *The Church and I: Woman's Responsibilities in the Church* (Scarborough, Ontario: Everyday Publications, 1979), 14.

31. Of course, such a "new interpretation of Scripture" results in new theology. For an example of such theology, with autobiographical details by the authors in the preface that correspond nicely with this pattern, see Stanley J. Grenz with Denise Muir Kjesbo, *Women in the Church: A Biblical Theology of Women in Ministry* (Downers Grove, Ill.: InterVarsity, 1995).

32. In one extreme instance, to which my wife was witness, several elders in a church of this sort confessed to uneasiness over the idea of women praying out loud in small group "house meetings" since they and their wives had understood the passages referring to silence, the headship of the husband in the home, and so on as forbidding the women to pray before adult male Christians. Thus, these men, well over sixty years old, had never heard their wives pray.

women; their entire preoccupation with the trivial in the life of the church, which has led to gossip or bickering over carpet colors, who slighted whom, and so on—have felt provoked to doubt the accuracy of this understanding of the biblical teaching on women's ministry in the church.

The third force from within is the evangelical commitment to world evangelization and the evident need for workers to further this cause. Clearly, there have never been enough men willing to do what has needed to be done. With the increasing education of women in Canada and the United States in the nineteenth and twentieth centuries, not only in theology but also in teaching, medicine, and other professions, the need for this skilled help has encouraged a rethinking of principles in order to get these women "on the field." Yet the relatively large number of Christian men "at home" apparently has kept this from challenging domestic practices in most instances. The increasing secularization of the culture, however, is bringing this sort of pressure to bear on the home front as well.

Indeed, a fourth pressure has come from outside. As women entered the workforce outside the home in the nineteenth and especially the twentieth century, more and more of them found it a shock to reenter the world of the church and find themselves treated in a way the outside world would condemn. Struggling as they have for equal rights, responsibilities, and dignity in the workplace, many evangelical women in particular have been disposed to find this construing of their role in the church backward and repressive. Many more have begun at least to question the traditional interpretation. For their part, men who have been sensitive to this struggle in the world have been alerted to the incongruity of this model in their churches.[33]

33. For examples of evangelicals wrestling with the messages they are receiving from society (particularly from the social sciences) and from the church, see the following: Mary Stewart Van Leeuwen, *Gender and Grace: Love, Work, and Parenting in a Changing World* (Downers Grove, Ill.: InterVarsity, 1990); Kaye Cook and Lance Lee, *Man and Woman: Alone and Together* (Wheaton, Ill.: BridgePoint, 1992); and Van Leeuwen, *After Eden.*

As other observers have noted, however, this experience of trends in the outside world has also had the opposite effect on some evangelicals. Many, alienated and frightened by the extremes of the secular feminist movement of the 1960s and 1970s, reacted by circumscribing further the roles of women in church and

Therefore, it has been precisely in seeing that women have exercised fruitful public ministries that paradigms of scriptural interpretation have been stretched, modified, and even rejected. To this has been added the pressure of negative effects of some of these models on women, the pressure of the commitment to world evangelization, and the pressure of women's experience in the workplace.

As this study indicates, model 1 has shown considerable resilience, stretching to embrace others of these options without breaking open into model 5. Yet the more model 1 includes exceptions, the more strain it is under, and the growing agreement among a significant number of evangelicals that women can exercise the same functions as men in the church no doubt owes much to the experiences of models 2, 3, and 4 even as it does simply to new ways of understanding Scripture.[34] Indeed, these experiences themselves often have been precisely the occasion for those new interpretations to develop.

---

parachurch organizations. But as the secular feminist movement has mellowed in recent years, with important leaders repudiating some of its earlier excesses, some of these evangelicals have felt freer to consider the issues again.

34. Howard A. Snyder and Daniel V. Runyon, among others, predicted that the number of women in public ministry among evangelical churches will continue to grow. See their *Foresight: Ten Major Trends That Will Dramatically Affect the Future of Christians and the Church* (Nashville: Nelson, 1986), 95–110. It is not clear what they would say now, almost twenty years later.

9

Why Johnny Can't Produce Christian Scholarship

A Reflection on Real-Life Impediments

I want to discuss a question many Christian scholars already can answer and about which many of us already complain. What we rarely do, however, is talk about this question in public and in an organized fashion. Our conversations instead tend to be conducted over lunch at an off-campus eatery after a frustrating faculty meeting or (more expansively) over drinks after a long day at an academic conference. I would like here to try to set out some observations and musings in this public way, in as orderly a fashion as I can manage.

I have found both guidance and stimulation concerning this matter in the research and reflections of three outstanding Christian scholars, historians George Marsden of Notre Dame and Mark Noll of Wheaton, and sociologist Robert Wuthnow of Princeton.[1] Their work helps to make clear that powerful historical, social, and psychological forces are at work in the academy and particularly in evangelical Christianity today that re-

1. George M. Marsden, "The Collapse of American Evangelical Academia," in *Faith and Rationality: Reason and Belief in God,* ed. Alvin Plantinga and Nicholas Wolterstorff (Notre Dame, Ind.: University of Notre Dame Press, 1983), 219–64; idem, *The Soul of the American University: From Protestant Establishment to Established Nonbelief* (New York/Oxford: Oxford University Press, 1994); Mark A. Noll, *The Scandal of the Evangelical Mind* (Grand Rapids: Eerdmans, 1994); Robert Wuthnow, "The Costs of Marginality," in *The Struggle for America's Soul: Evangelicals, Liberals, and Secularism* (Grand Rapids: Eerdmans, 1989), 158–76; and idem, "Living the Question: Evangelical Christianity and Critical Thought," *Cross Currents* (summer 1990): 160–75.

sist and retard Christian scholarship, and that these must be recognized to rectify the situation. I trust that the conclusions offered here about evangelicals (the Christian scholars I know best) will be useful for other Christian scholars to consider as well.

Let us first understand that only a minority of postsecondary teachers of *any* stripe produces much scholarship at all. Two different sources give us a sense of the situation. First, Wuthnow describes what is known as "Lotka's Law." Wuthnow says that the number of people who produce a particular number of articles in a given time period is geometrically inversely proportional to the latter number. More precisely:

> For any discipline with a total given number of members who produce one article in a given period, the number of people in that discipline who will produce N articles in the same period is proportional to one divided by N-squared. Thus in a discipline such as sociology with no more than about 5,000 members with full-time jobs in academic institutions, the number of active researchers who produce, say, three articles a year will be about 550 [that is, 5,000/9] and the number who produce four articles will be about 300 [that is, 5,000/16], if we assume that all 5,000 produce at least one article every year.[2]

The *Chronicle of Higher Education*'s almanac, however, makes this last assumption dubious, at least for academicians in general. Over 35,000 faculty members at almost 400 postsecondary institutions in the United States—including two-year colleges, four-year colleges, and universities (both public and private in each case)—were polled on a wide range of questions during the academic year 1989–90.[3] In this poll, more than 45 percent of the faculty members had not had one piece of professional writing accepted for publication or published in the last *two* years. And one must not presume that the faculty members of the two-year colleges were primarily responsible for the low averages. For four-year private colleges, the "nones" totaled 52

2. Wuthnow, "Costs of Marginality," 164.
3. The editors of the *Chronicle of Higher Education, The Almanac of Higher Education 1995* (Chicago/London: University of Chicago Press, 1995), 60–61.

percent, and for the public ones, 43 percent. Only at the universities were things significantly better: At the public ones, 22 percent claimed "none," and at the private, less than 16 percent. Still, this means that at the public universities better than one in five faculty members claimed no publication of a professional piece of writing or an acceptance for publication over a two-year period, and the ratio was one in six at the private universities.

How about Wuthnow's baseline of at least one publication per year? If one were publishing one article per year, then one would have published two articles in the previous two years and would have had at least one article accepted for publication in the coming year (given the time it takes for most journals to referee and publish an article). Even if we are generous and presume that the poll's term "professional writing" means an article or a book, not just a research note or a book review, we must look for averages of 3 or more over the previous two years. The poll total of such baseline scholars or better is only 29 percent. At the universities, the number of "baseline or better" is 51 percent (public) and 58 percent (private). Almost half of the public university scholars and more than one-third of the private university scholars do not meet Wuthnow's basic standard of one article per year—presuming, again, that the poll does not count reviews or notes (which it probably does). An interesting question, then, one we will not attempt to answer here directly, is Why don't *most* scholars produce very much?

The title of this chapter and the subsequent headings play off the well-known book by R. F. Flesch, *Why Johnny Can't Read— and What You Can Do about It*.[4] I do not intend to ignore the question of why "Joanna" can't produce Christian scholarship: Indeed, I address the question of gender directly later in the essay. Let's proceed, then, to consider why Johnny can't produce Christian scholarship, letting the psychoanalysts in the crowd sort out how often this discussion of Johnny the scholar is, in fact, autobiographical!

---

4. R. F. Flesch, *Why Johnny Can't Read—and What You Can Do about It* (New York: Harper, 1955).

Problems with Johnny

Because Johnny Is Insufficiently Educated

By the end of the 1980s, Wuthnow could gather data that suggested that what he called "conservative" and "liberal" Christians were "virtually indistinguishable in terms of education."[5] Later in the same article in which he reports this finding, however, Wuthnow points out that distinctions in fact continue to mark especially those who have advanced into the realm of postsecondary education. From his vantage at Princeton University, Wuthnow observes that social class continues to play a large part within the academic community. This, he sharply asserts, is a dirty little secret academics of many stripes prefer to cover up.

The North American academy, after all, purports to be a pure meritocracy. Those who succeed within it, so we professors like to say, do so according to their own accomplishments. Those of us with privileged backgrounds especially work to propagate this myth of the self-made man or woman: I earned every degree, every accomplishment, and every accolade. Yet, Wuthnow counters:

> Despite all the talk about financial aid, it is no accident that a high proportion of students at places like Princeton have gone to expensive private high schools, enjoyed summers abroad or received tutoring at the finest academies. Nor is it an accident that these students continue on to graduate schools and academic posts in disproportionate numbers.[6]

Academically minded homes more likely produce academically minded children, and well-to-do homes provide resources for aspiring students that less-well-off homes cannot. Evangelicals, according to Wuthnow, tend not to come from the elite classes of society and thus either do not produce academically minded children in the first place or might produce them but lack the resources and interest to cultivate them to compete and succeed in the leading arenas of academic endeavor.

5. Wuthnow, "Living the Question," 164.
6. Ibid., 173. For a more recent portrait of Princeton students, see David Brooks, "The Organization Kid," *The Atlantic Monthly* 287 (April 2001): 40–54.

Indeed, says Wuthnow, this class reality affects even the exceptional evangelical student who actually does succeed in gaining entrance to a first-rate doctoral program, the stepping-stone to professional success:

> Once embarked on advanced studies, the evangelical student from a typical background is also likely to face a number of continuing obstacles: inadequate foreign language training, which prolongs the years of study; the need to support a spouse and, perhaps, children, which reflects the evangelical dating and mating subculture; and a pragmatic working-class orientation, which extols finishing quickly and getting a job rather than taking the intellectual risks that someone of more affluent means can afford.[7]

I believe Wuthnow's observations are true, but they are less true of each age group counting down from professors now at retirement age. That is, because upward mobility has affected the evangelical subcultures, I expect that this difference will be less and less marked in each new wave of graduate students. It is also true that those who come from less privileged backgrounds sometimes succeed in academia precisely because they are used to struggle, to working hard, to earning everything they get. They simply have a better work ethic than some who come from softer, easier homes. Still, the importance of this combination of financial and moral support can hardly be overestimated, nor can the corollary importance of the lack of such a combination.

Because Johnny Is Dogmatic

Because Johnny comes from a subculture that is treated as if it were a cognitive minority in the academy, and often (as we will discuss further later) a despised and misunderstood one at that, he might have grown up to think and act with unusual adaptability as he negotiates the world of higher learning. Such flexibility might be a positive advantage in the academy. Alas, however, if the intellectual portrait of evangelicals painted by Noll and others is correct, it is more likely that Johnny instead has been schooled in a defensive—and sometimes offensive—dogmatism.

7. Wuthnow, "Living the Question," 174.

By this I mean more than an unyielding defense of articles of Christian faith and practice. But let us not move past this particular point too quickly, for in the mind of the conservative or fundamentalist evangelical, virtually everything counts as a matter of Christian faith and practice and cannot be debated, much less yielded. Thus, some evangelical students have trouble countenancing alternatives to creation science, hierarchical gender roles, or the Mosaic authorship of the Pentateuch, since all of these have been taught to them as matters of faith and practice.

Maintaining a commitment to so many articles of faith and practice tends to breed a rather rigid and clear-cut outlook in other respects as well. (I have found both as an evangelical churchman and as a university teacher of such students.) Perhaps this is why I have formed the impression (as have other observers such as Marsden and Noll) that when evangelicals actually do attend university, they tend to show up in the natural sciences, in engineering schools and colleges of medicine, nursing, pharmacy, and rehabilitation therapy, rather than in the humanities, social sciences, and law. Ambiguity, process, tentative conclusions, and continual argument all are endemic to the latter disciplines, and evangelicals may not be well disposed to them. Much better to be in a field in which everyone agrees at least roughly on what a 20 mm bolt is, or how to diagnose rheumatic fever, or when to take the crucible out of the kiln. Indeed, I propose that there is a kind of twofold Law of Evangelical Incidence here: Evangelicals are present in a discipline in inverse proportion to the amount of (1) ambiguity and (2) ideological conflict present in that discipline.

To be sure, I risk oversimplification here, since it is true that conducting first-order research in the natural and applied sciences is also a matter of creativity, doubt, dispute, and provisionality. So then I ask, how many evangelicals go on from undergraduate degrees in science or the applied sciences to *research*, rather than to professional, positions in those fields?

Because Johnny Is Afraid

Johnny comes to academic work afraid because his subculture has taught him (with more than a grain of truth) that intellectual inquiry can threaten one's faith. What his subculture has not taught him, however, are the benefits of "constructive doubt," of the reexamination of inherited truths and the personal appropriation of them through reflection. Thus, he proceeds defensively through his education, never able to sympathize with other points of view that might well enrich his own, even if only in stimulating opposition. Such a stance is unlikely to lead to academic curiosity, much less to success.

A different Johnny might be afraid in another direction: of being found out as someone with a dark, that is to say, "evangelical," past. If Johnny has spent any length of time in the university, especially among its leading lights as a graduate student and professor, he knows that owning an evangelical heritage is no advantage and quite possibly a disadvantage. Furthermore, he does not need others to tell him this. He probably feels considerable ambivalence and even anger over his anti-intellectual background and thus perhaps does all he can to cover it in the presence of those he now wishes to impress. The last thing he wants to do, then, is to conduct his research in any way that might provide a clue to his Christian past and, if he has maintained it, his current Christian faith.

Because Johnny Has Caved In or Sold Out

Perhaps this fear of Johnny's leads him in fact to capitulate to the reigning orthodoxies of his field. After all, a guy's gotta make a living, and it does no good for some misguided evangelical Don Quixote to tilt at the windmills of intellectual fashion. By now, Johnny has gotten used to the queasy feeling in his stomach as he keeps silent when his fellow scholars disparage the integrity of religion and of Christianity in particular. He has accustomed himself to having certain questions in his own mind either ridiculed or, more likely, never brought up at all in academic discourse. He gets along by going along. Thus, he radically bifurcates his professional and religious lives so that the left hand of his university life knows nothing of what he does with his right hand at home and at church.

Perhaps Johnny has gone a significant step further. Perhaps he is so disappointed with his heritage and so enthralled with other ideologies that he adopts the latter wholesale, at least in his professional life. He does not just hide behind Marxist or feminist or deconstructionist or pluralist approaches: He revels in them and champions them in all his work without ever submitting them to a Christian critique. Johnny might be a churchgoer. Johnny might even teach at a Christian college. But his work is thoroughly untouched by significant Christian principles, indistinguishable from work done by a non-Christian elsewhere. And since this might well benefit Johnny's academic profile in the guild at large—and also perhaps, ironically enough, in his own Christian college—he has powerful reasons not to second-guess what he does. In sum, we might well encounter here the common figure of the evangelical who is more liberal than the liberals and more worldly than the worldly as Johnny loudly asserts to them, and to himself, his emancipation from his past.

Because Joanna Is a Woman

In these days of affirmative action and job-equity programs, it would normally be a significant advantage for Johnny to be a female academic: "Joanna." But if Joanna is an evangelical, she likely will never get to compete for an academic job in the first place. Because of the gender roles that continue to prevail in North American evangelicalism, she will be subject to a constant, even "atmospheric," pressure to train for particular professions such as teaching or social work or, perhaps, a medical field—and, of course, to get married and bear children. Given the evangelical preoccupation with "focusing on the family," any young woman who expresses an interest in graduate work and a professor's job a decade or more down the road from her undergraduate matriculation will receive even less approbation than does her male evangelical counterpart.

I know this firsthand from counseling academically gifted women at several colleges and universities. On the one hand, I tell them, they will be able to compete better against men once they have their education in hand because of affirmative action. On the other hand, I tell them, they will have to endure strong social pressures to take another course. And if they want children, as most of them do, they will have to face the questions that confront every professional woman: Who will rear the children, especially during their first few years? Who will support the family? How can your degree be interrupted, for how long, and at what final cost? And if she is an assistant professor, she will be asked, How can you act as if you are on some kind of "mommy track" when the tenure clock ticks the same for you as it does for someone who is not the primary caregiver?

Problems with Johnny's Job

Additional problems, as intimated already, have nothing to do with Johnny himself. These problems are external to Johnny, and some are quite severe.

Because of Johnny's Teaching Responsibilities

It is likely that Johnny, if he is now Dr. Johnny and has gained a professorship somewhere, is teaching at a Christian college. In Canada, to be sure, it is more likely than in the United States that he is at a public university, given the small number of Christian universities in Canada. Let us consider both situations.

If Johnny is at a typical Christian college, he has at least four courses to teach all the time.[8] In a relatively few schools, he teaches three at a time. A typical university load is two or perhaps three courses at a time, and a load is even less at the most research-oriented institutions. In this regard, Wuthnow affirms that time for research is the single resource least available to would-be researchers in Christian colleges, since relatively heavy teaching loads crowd it out.[9]

What *kind* of teaching Johnny does also makes a difference. In many Christian colleges, professors spend most of their time teaching introductory courses at the first- and second-year levels. Furthermore, they have no graduate courses in which to teach cutting-

8. Michael S. Hamilton, a scholar who (with Nathan O. Hatch of Notre Dame University) has researched such matters, estimates that roughly 85 percent of members of the Coalition for Christian Colleges and Universities have at least a four-and-four teaching load (personal correspondence with the author via electronic mail, 5 July 1995).

9. "Much of the reason for [the concentration of research output in relatively few individual scholars] is that the resources necessary to do research—especially time—are limited to those in a small number of institutions" (Wuthnow, "Costs of Marginality," 164).

edge findings in their specialties. To be sure, teaching introductory courses offers great benefits to one's teaching: It presses one to be simple and clear. But a steady regimen of such teaching can keep one from developing the ability to be profound and precise. Moreover, introductory students by definition can offer less extensive critique (although sometimes much more stimulating than one might expect or be prepared for!) than advanced students.

If Johnny teaches at a secular university, he faces different challenges. One of the benefits of teaching at a Christian institution is that one is expected (or ought to be expected!) to present one's discipline in concert with the express Christian commitments of the school. At a secular university, however, Johnny must be careful not to offend easily aggrieved constituencies by appearing to favor any one religion or ideology over another. This reality offers the benefit of encouraging him to learn how to speak carefully and respectfully in a pluralistic situation. Unfortunately, it can also press him either to withdraw cautiously into safe, mealymouthed platitudes or to jump on the current ideological bandwagon.

Second, the teaching loads at public universities are not necessarily better than at private Christian colleges. He may teach fewer courses at the former than at the latter—although the gap, I expect, will narrow as money continues to disappear from public institutions of all sorts—but the class sizes can differ tremendously. Public universities routinely offer courses in science and social science that enroll hundreds of students. In the university department in which I used to teach, each section of the introductory course in world religions (hardly the most popular of first-year arts offerings) regularly exceeded eighty students. Teaching assistance for such courses is disappearing as funds dry up for graduate students, and the graduate students themselves, therefore, are finding it more and more difficult to finance an education even as they face no encouraging job prospects waiting at the other end. Thus, graduate courses sometimes go begging for enrollments, and professors have to "pick up" a section of a popular introductory course instead. Furthermore, only in some institutions do professors get significant "teaching credit" for supervising graduate theses. Most simply guide theses "on load"—that is, as part of their somewhat nebulous list of job expectations.

In both kinds of institutions, therefore, there are obstacles to scholarship for *anyone*, and some extra ones for evangelicals.

Because of Johnny's School's Constituency

Professors recognize that at most colleges and universities that offer tenure there is a rule: up or out. In other words, when you apply for tenure, either you are granted tenure and usually promoted to associate professor (hence "up") or you are given a one-year contract to find a new job before you are fired (hence "out"). And while teaching ability is important, research output is also key to a successful application in most schools. There is another old saying, therefore, that every young professor keeps before himself or herself as the tenure application deadline looms: publish or perish.

If Johnny is at a secular institution, therefore, he might be especially careful to conform his research to what will succeed in the market and especially to what will impress his departmental colleagues who have the most say in whether the school offers him tenure. This is hardly a situation conducive to bold, critical Christian thinking.

If Johnny is at a Christian institution, however, he has the opposite problem. If his bold, critical Christian thinking—something one would hope his school would approve—happens to lead him to question certain dogmas of his tradition's faith, to inquire into certain embarrassing inconsistencies in his tradition's history, or to challenge the sacredness of certain cows venerated by his tradition's powerful elders or grassroots supporters, then the old saying dramatically changes by one word: publish *and* perish! Indeed, the instances can be multiplied of evangelical professors who for years taught certain things in their classrooms without getting into trouble with their immediate superiors but who, when they took their ideas to the public through print, were adjudged too hot to handle and were moved out.

Thus, we have the vexed question of academic freedom in both secular and Christian contexts. Freedom for whom, to do what, on whose behalf? The irony is that in both contexts there are serious constraints on Johnny's work as a Christian scholar.

Because of Johnny's Pay and Other Funding

If Johnny teaches at a Christian school, the odds are good that he is paid barely a living wage—unless he is a senior faculty member. I have little hard evidence for this but mental files full of anecdotes! Thus, he has little money to finance his research— to fund a laboratory or personal library, to hire student assistants, to attend academic meetings, to consult with other scholars, or to conduct field research. At most secular universities, the salary situation has also deteriorated significantly since the late 1960s. Most junior professors at most universities in North America, for example, can barely afford a modest house, if they can afford one at all, and they may well never be able to afford a house and other amenities if they want to reside within a half hour's commuting distance of their schools.

It is essential, therefore, that professors acquire funds for research. Christian colleges typically offer little internal support to their faculty. Secular universities might offer more (better libraries, for instance), but most funding for research there, too, must come from outside. If an evangelical scholar has not acquired a strong academic pedigree and developed a significant network of influential acquaintances (with the latter significantly depending on the former, especially in the first decade of a scholar's professional life), then it is unlikely that he or she will secure the first grant that funds the research that produces the results that justifies the second grant and so on. With large teaching responsibilities (plus extracurricular work often demanded by administrations and development offices, particularly at Christian schools), younger faculty can be in a catch-22 situation from which they can never emerge. All of this is in play before we begin to examine the prejudices that might greet an application from a scholar teaching at an obviously Christian school who applies to the normal secular granting agencies in his or her field.

Problems with Johnny's Peers

Because Others Fear, Despise, or Misunderstand Johnny

Wuthnow and Marsden have both declared publicly that conservative Christians, whether Roman Catholic or Protestant, are

the last remaining politically correct targets for abuse and neglect in the contemporary academy.[10] Wuthnow savages the
Chronicle of Higher Education, for instance, for featuring writing
by "naive journalists [who] can scarcely distinguish a Christian
from a Jew, let alone an evangelical from a fundamentalist."[11]
This ignorance is bad enough, he continues, but evangelicals and
fundamentalists regularly are mistreated in the secular media
and academy. Why is this so, he asks. He answers his own question thus:

> Because evangelicalism is not a reality that outsiders have tried
> seriously to understand; it is a symbol for all the fears that main-
> stream scholars and intellectuals worry about most. Evangeli-
> calism is taboo because it conjures up images of crazed cult
> members burning books, closing their minds to rational argu-
> ment, and allowing charismatic leaders to rape their intellects.
> In a society that values higher education as much as ours, the
> mind is our most cherished resource. To waste a mind is, as we
> say, a terrible thing. Drugs and evangelicalism stand for the
> same thing—the loss of a human mind.[12]

I have encountered this prejudice—for prejudice is what it
is—many times. From my undergraduate days to teaching at
my own university, from talking with strangers on an airplane
to being interviewed by secular media reporters, again and
again I encounter the same reaction: "You say (openly!) that
you are a Christian, and yet you seem, well, *intelligent* and even
have a sense of humor! How can these things be?!" (More particular stereotypes have also been my curse: I am a male evangelical, so I must be a misogynist; I am a white evangelical, so I
must be a racist; I am a middle-class evangelical, so I must be
politically right-wing.)

As Wuthnow points out, the particular shame for evangelicals
in the academy lies in the fact that they *choose* to be evangelicals.
Unlike, say, blacks or women or Jews, evangelicals *could be otherwise and choose not to be.* Surely, then, they must be too be-

10. This is a theme in Marsden's "Concluding Unscientific Postscript" to
Soul of the American University, 429–44.
11. Wuthnow, "Living the Question," 164.
12. Ibid., 171.

nighted to realize the intellectual inadequacy (to put it mildly) of their convictions and thereby are demonstrably intellectually inferior. African-American studies, women's studies, and Jewish studies all make sense. But only as an example of psychosocial pathology would "evangelical studies" appear on a curriculum.[13]

Problems with the Task Itself

As if the foregoing personal, psychological, and sociological dynamics weren't enough, there are at least two major problems attached to the task of Christian scholarship itself.

Because It Is More than Twice as Hard

Theologian George Lindbeck has written that embracing a religion is, among other things, like learning a language as part of entering a community shaped by and continuing to shape that language.[14] Responsible evangelical scholars nowadays must engage, therefore, in the extraordinary fourfold task of (1) learning their own language, and all that goes with it, as Christians; (2) learning the language(s), and all that goes with them, of contemporary scholarship in their field; (3) learning to translate between the two; and (4) going beyond this to fruitfully engage the two. It is much easier to grow up in an intellectual environment utterly at ease in the modern academy: You can remain monolingual. But Christians are citizens of two realms and speak at least two languages, and successful scholars must become fluent in both and masters of integrating the two.

Sadly, many Christian scholars become fluent only in the language and culture of the academy. They normally have to do so to earn a respectable Ph.D. But their understanding of Christianity lags behind in an elementary form, utterly unequal as an intellectual conversation partner in their own heads, much less as a reliable and resourceful guide for advanced inquiry. Other Christians become fluent in the language of the church but fail to become

13. Ibid., 171–73.
14. This is a basic theme in George A. Lindbeck, *The Nature of Doctrine: Religion and Theology in a Postliberal Age* (Philadelphia: Westminster, 1984).

adept in the discourse of the academy. They might struggle through a Ph.D., learning enough of its literatures and lore to pass (just as they struggle through their German or Greek exams), but then they retreat into a Christian ghetto and relax, without ever again seriously encountering that other set of cultures.

Frankly, it *is* difficult to be a thoroughly Christian scholar— to be thoroughly Christian, thoroughly a scholar, and then thoroughly a Christian scholar. One wonders, then, about the wisdom of Christian colleges and universities hiring faculty members with reputable graduate degrees in their fields but little or no substantial preparation in Christian thought as a complement and counterpart to their thorough immersion in the cultures of the academic discipline. Will a faculty seminar or two on "the integration of faith and learning" make up the difference? Consider the opposite. Would a theologian be fit to teach sociology prepared only by a faculty seminar or two on the social sciences, plus reading or hearing addresses on pop sociology once or twice each weekend as a sort of parallel to the way Christians hear sermons?

If my construal of this task of thoroughly Christian scholarship is reasonably accurate, then the Christian scholar is at a disadvantage compared to the scholar who is at ease in the secular academy, for the Christian scholar must work more than twice as hard. Still, that challenge is the same for any missionary, for any foreigner or pilgrim in a strange land, and it simply must be recognized and taken on by the serious Christian scholar.

Because Few Will Thank Johnny for It

Suppose Johnny is a budding evangelical scholar who hears that few will thank him for his scholarly work, but he is not utterly discouraged by this fact. The final reality is this: If he undertakes the onerous task of preparing for and then prosecuting a career in authentic and ambitious Christian scholarship, he must be prepared for little praise. Christians will misunderstand him, especially most evangelical Christians. They will not appreciate his successes, and they will wonder, sometimes out loud, why he doesn't help out at the church more, or write for the denominational magazine, or teach the youth group. What, they will inquire, is he doing for the kingdom of God? Most of his non-Christian counterparts will either remain completely unappreciative of any integrated work he does or actively resist the signs of a distinct Christian influence in his scholarship. Why in the world, they might ask, is he compromising what is otherwise a promising line of inquiry with that medieval drivel? Is he perhaps less than he appears?

Some Christians, thank God, will approve and bless him. And some non-Christians will catch on and admire him. And, not to put too fine a point on it, who cares anyway? Christian scholars are, finally, just Christians who look ahead to a much more important assessment, a final examination that makes all of these intervening evaluations disappear in its bright glory. Even Christian scholars, and especially Christian scholars, are to set their minds on things above, where Christ is.

What Can Be Done

What Johnny Can Do

Johnny cannot help his upbringing. If he was raised as an evangelical, however, he has firsthand acquaintance with a subculture that, despite an explosion of scholarly study in the last several decades, continues to require explanation to itself and to others. As a result, Johnny might well be able to conduct research in his particular discipline on evangelicals and evangelicalism.[15]

This leads to a broader principle: Bloom where you are planted. Study what lies within reach of your resources of time and money. Perhaps your dream of working with a particle accelerator will never be realized. Perhaps you will never get money to travel to archives in France or Japan. What can you study instead? Christians must forthrightly consider their doctrine of providence: Has God made a terrible mistake in locating you where he did, so that nothing can be done until he fixes things and moves you out?

Speaking of location, Johnny would do well not to believe that the grass is greener in every respect at the intellectual cen-

15. Wuthnow makes a number of helpful suggestions for the social sciences in this regard in "Costs of Marginality," 168–76.

ter of his field. In the center is where the paradigms of the moment reign supreme, and those working in them are most heavily invested, naturally, in maintaining them. On the margins, however, in smaller or less prestigious schools that are less concerned and less able to be utterly *au courant,* there can be a correspondingly greater freedom for creativity. It is a truism that important innovation often comes from the margins, not from the center.

What is true of social location, moreover, can also be true of intellectual location. Some of Johnny's dogmatism, some of his refusal to yield articles of faith simply because a powerful figure in his academic field summons him to do so, might not only keep him theologically orthodox but also help him to maintain an important psychological distance from the reigning "orthodoxies" in his discipline. Precisely because evangelicals are not entirely at ease in their fields' discourses, precisely because evangelicals are used to the dynamic of being "in" but not entirely "of," they can capitalize on their habitual posture of difference by exploiting it. They can consider new angles of vision, currently forgotten wisdom from the past, or overlooked data that spoils the reigning paradigm and points forward to a new model. It is not merely sour grapes for evangelicals to believe that being at the center is not always best if one's goal is to make a genuine and original contribution, rather than merely to be recognized.

Third, Johnny needs to consider how much of his occupational calling is to research and how much is to teaching and institutional or community service. Since any of these tasks can consume all of one's available time, compromise is necessary no matter what ratio one works out. Perhaps Johnny in fact has been called by God primarily to teaching and not to scholarship beyond keeping abreast of developments in his teaching field so as to keep his lectures fresh.

Perhaps, though, Johnny needs to consider whether he needs to devote more time to research and writing and become more efficient in his teaching and other service. Indeed, to be true to his calling as a research scholar, he must curtail involvements in both of these other areas. I shall invoke here the advice given to me by an accomplished older scholar who had attained the rank of full professor at a prominent university while winning a teaching award along the way. He told me frankly, "I should have concentrated more on research and less on teaching. Compromise your teaching in order to conduct research."

I know he did not mean to neglect teaching! What he recognized, however, is that teaching demands are always there, always immediate. Research seems infinitely deferrable, at least until tenure and promotion dates suddenly loom. And no one else—not students, not colleagues, not department chairs, not deans, not alumni—will care about your research nearly as much as you do: At one time or another they will all want you to do something else. Johnny, in this respect, has to look, perhaps ruthlessly, for ways to increase time in his schedule for research. He regularly has to shut his office door or hide in a library carrel, hole up for hours on end, and do what he believes God has called him to do. And perhaps he can help certain colleagues and students to see that such pursuits are an authentic part of his calling too.

What Johnny's Church Can Do

Precious few academicians are ever going to live with the economic comfort enjoyed by those first employed in the boom of the 1960s and early 1970s—although in some Christian colleges, commendably, faculty salaries have never been better. Costs of first-rate training are high, and prospective salaries are relatively low. Strategically minded churches, therefore, need to begin to sponsor excellent students through the best possible graduate training, just as they sponsor workers in other professions for which the cost is high and the expected wages low (such as pastors and missionaries). To be sure, most church members will need to be taught to appreciate the importance of academic vocations, as they do ecclesiastical ones. And most people outside the academy will need to understand the economic realities of academic life today, which are contrary to the widespread myth of the well-paid, underworked professor of leisure. This is one problem, however, that can be helped largely by throwing money at it, and churches need to consider doing so.

Second, churches can pray for such scholars, both in the challenges of their student days and in their work as professionals. Yes, too much can be made of academic pursuits, especially by academicians! Our jobs are not in fact more glorious in the work of God than others'. But many of our churches deprecate the intellectual sphere and ignore the strategic importance of academic work. We need to help our churches see that *someone* is going to be producing the research and writing the textbooks that will influence tomorrow's members of Congress or Parliament, tomorrow's journalists, tomorrow's teachers, tomorrow's film directors, tomorrow's executives, tomorrow's cultural leaders. Christians ought to be salt and light in those enterprises. Churches, therefore, can spiritually, as well as financially, support their members in such pursuits.

What Johnny's School Can Do

Christian colleges can reconsider their historic practice of hiring faculty members with bona fide expertise in one or another academic discipline and no demonstrable academic expertise in the Christian religion. Such colleges can decide whether they need to insist on at least some solid academic preparation in Christian thought that will make the integration of faith and learning more a correlation of equal partners. As a stopgap measure, such colleges should consider insisting on rigorous and regular faculty seminars to ensure at least minimal theological, philosophical, and historical literacy on which specialists can then build a strong Christian understanding of each particular discipline.[16]

Once hired, faculty can sign individualized contracts that will help them make the most of their gifts and interests—a basic biblical principle. Some faculty members want to concentrate on teaching, others on research. Contracts can be drawn up to specify expectations each year and over several years so that individuals can fulfill their vocations best without any misunderstanding that they are shirking one or another dimension of their duties.[17]

Colleges and universities can raise money from donors to supplement research funds obtained through granting agencies.

16. I am informed by Dean Michael Wilkins of Biola University that his institution embarked on precisely such a program of annual seminars, beginning in 1994 (personal correspondence).

17. I experienced such a beneficent program at Northwestern College, Iowa, under Deans Harold Heie and Robert Zwier, 1987–90.

Often money is raised for building or other more attractive programs. But colleges (and I think especially of Christian colleges here) need to take on the task of exciting their alumni and other constituents about the importance of research. What gets discussed and praised in the alumni publications, for example, or in the school catalogue and at special recruiting events?

Colleges and universities can train their faculty in more effective grant applications. Many major universities pay a full-time staff to help professors succeed in such fund-raising, realizing that even a few successes easily pay for the cost of such an office. Such institutions, and perhaps also the Christian scholarly societies, can also deliberately and programmatically encourage the linkage of junior with senior scholars, within the school and without, so as to cultivate each new generation of scholars.

Finally, and most generally, colleges and universities can look hard at their own sense of mission and the structures in which they have placed their faculty members. Is there incongruity between the one and the other? Does a particular college need to consider whether it is called by God or by society at large to generate new knowledge through research, as well as to transmit knowledge through teaching? Committee work, student hours, development obligations, and so on all need to be scrutinized in the light of this goal: to enable at least some of the school's professors to make an impact on their fields, even as they are hired to teach them.

At last, it all comes down to this. Are evangelical professors, evangelical churches, and evangelical schools truly committed to shaping intellectual fields according to Christian principles, to exerting Christian influence on the contemporary mind not only through teaching but also through published scholarship? If we are not so committed, let us set aside our pretenses and honestly take our rightful place in the academic hierarchy. If we *are* so committed, though, let us be committed heart and soul, mind and strength, datebook and checkbook. The task deserves, and requires, no less.

10

Evangelical Theology Should Be Evangelical

A Conservative, Radical Proposal

Evangelical theology is not a popular cause these days. In many evangelical churches, theology of any stripe is something for which apologies are rendered from the pulpit whenever an intrepid preacher ventures onto its turf. Among some evangelicals, theology is something to be held up for amusement or scorn, as the silly games of underemployed and slothful intellectuals. Or theology is something to be feared as an abyss of dangerous speculation in which one's traditional faith can be torn apart in the crosscurrents of divergent and even antagonistic streams of thought.

Having attended my share of professional theological conferences and read more than a few books of academic theology, I confess to some sympathy with these attitudes. But such antipathies hardly serve to encourage the work of evangelical theology.

The situation for evangelical theology is actually even worse than this, however, for trouble lies even within the ranks of the theologians. Nowadays evangelical theologians over here are enamored with Karl Barth, or over there by his latter-day saints, the postliberals. Some evangelicals currently explore intellectual trajectories farther, along which have traveled the theologians of process, while others seek wisdom from the ancient Eastern churches. Some evangelicals find both stimulation and stability in the first millennium, while others seek it in early modern Reformed scholasticism. And some few evangelicals work creatively in liberationist, feminist, and postmodern modes.

Evangelicals these days, then, seem to be looking interestedly at what almost everyone else is doing in theology. This openness to learn from other Christians is to be commended, particularly as one considers the confessional or fundamentalist blinkers many of these brothers and sisters have labored to shed. Still, however, the evangelical tradition itself stimulates precious little creative work within evangelicalism and virtually none, to my knowledge at least, from without. While evangelicals around the world rejoice as millions of people convert to their form of Christianity, there are few theologians of stature who have converted to evangelical theology from some other tradition and now work within it.[1] And even if I have overlooked a notable convert or two, to look for converts is to miss the larger point. Evangelicals can and do explore Ruether, or Hartshorne, or Zizioulas, or Gutiérrez in order to enrich their evangelicalism. But which liberals, neo-orthodox, Roman Catholics, or what-have-you take the evangelical tradition seriously as a theological resource even to enrich their own perspectives?

Whether or not anyone else takes notice, however, I suggest that the evangelical tradition itself continues to offer good gifts to evangelical theologians today. And I do not mean merely that this or that overlooked or forgotten evangelical theologian deserves greater attention—although it is gratifying to see attention paid to Jonathan Edwards and increasing attention paid to Adolf Schlatter, to mention just two worthy examples from the past. I mean that the evangelical tradition itself provides a stance in which theology can be ably and helpfully undertaken in our time. It is, I would now like to contend at some length, a stance that both guards against some of the dangers of contemporary theology and guides toward the benefit of all those who study the theology it produces.

1. Among this small company might be numbered Alister McGrath, Royce Gruenler, and Tom Oden, depending on one's definition of evangelical. See Michael Bauman, "Alister McGrath," in *Handbook of Evangelical Theologians*, ed. Walter A. Elwell (Grand Rapids: Baker, 1993), 445–47; Royce Gordon Gruenler, *The Inexhaustible God: Biblical Faith and the Challenge of Process Theism* (Grand Rapids: Baker, 1983); and Thomas C. Oden, *Systematic Theology*, 3 vols. (San Francisco: HarperSanFrancisco, 1992, 1994).

What Is "Evangelical"?

It is an irony that in a tradition that prizes plain, clear speech, the very word *evangelical* is patient of at least half a dozen definitions, and some of those are hotly contested by interested parties within and without any particular form of evangelicalism. Recognizing that "evangelical" can indeed denote anything having to do with the gospel, people generally trace evangelicalism as a distinct tradition in Christianity to the eighteenth-century revivals on both sides of the Atlantic Ocean, led by eminences such as George Whitefield, John and Charles Wesley, and Jonathan Edwards. If we take this range of interconnected revivals as our benchmark for the evangelical tradition, we can induce a list of five characteristics. And such a list enjoys the approval of most historians and theologians who study evangelicalism.[2]

First, evangelicals believe and champion the gospel of God's work of salvation and particularly as it is focused in the person of Jesus Christ. Even more particularly, evangelicals teach and delight in the incarnation of the Lord and in his inauguration of the kingdom of God, but they pay special attention—as they believe the Bible itself does—to the death and resurrection of Christ as together constituting the central event of God's redemptive project. Christ, therefore, is worshiped as the Son of God, venerated as the center of history, followed as the model of righteousness, and looked for as the promised deliverer who will return someday in power to consummate salvation history.

Second, evangelicals believe and champion the Bible as the uniquely authoritative rendition of God's Word in words to us. Evangelicals appreciate that the Bible is a mysterious book in many ways and disagree on how to interpret it and thus what it says in each respect. But evangelicals agree that, while one can be puzzled by the Bible, the faithful Christian cannot disagree with it. As God's Spirit illuminates and commends it to God's

2. For a more thorough discussion of definition, see David W. Bebbington, *Evangelicalism in Modern Britain: A History from the 1730s to the 1980s* (London: Unwin Hyman, 1989), 1–19; George M. Marsden, "Introduction," in *Evangelicalism and Modern America*, ed. George M. Marsden (Grand Rapids: Eerdmans, 1984), viii–xvi; and John G. Stackhouse, Jr., *Canadian Evangelicalism in the Twentieth Century: An Introduction to Its Character* (Toronto: University of Toronto Press, 1993), 6–12.

people, their response to such teaching must be gratitude and obedience.

Third, evangelicals believe and champion conversion as the correct way to describe God's work of salvation in each Christian and as a reality to be experienced, not merely affirmed. Evangelicals, that is, believe that each person must be born again by the renewing power of the Holy Spirit—although evangelicals disagree on just how evident this renewal will be at any given time in the process. And then each Christian must go on to mature in growing conformity to the pattern of Christ's own devotion to God. Conversion, that is, denotes both the moment of new birth and the lifetime of transformation that follows as the Holy Spirit prepares us for eternity with God.

Fourth, evangelicals believe and champion mission as the chief goal of Christian life on earth. At times, such activism in seeking to bring to others both the message of salvation and the charity of Christ has meant that evangelicals have paid relatively less attention to worship, theology, the cultivation of the earth, or other expressions of the well-rounded Christian life. Still, evangelicals affirm that Christ has built the church on earth and maintains it here not merely, or even primarily, to praise, to think, or to garden, but to make disciples.

Fifth, evangelicals believe and champion these four elements of the generic Christian tradition in ways that other traditions do not. To be sure, all branches of the orthodox Christian faith affirm the story of salvation centering on Christ, the authority of the Bible as God's written Word (even as some place other authorities alongside it), the necessity of conversion, and the call to mission. There is nothing peculiarly evangelical in any of these four convictions. But evangelicals place special emphasis on this constellation of four and do so in such a way as to relativize every other conviction. There is nothing in the generic evangelical impulse that militates directly against denominational distinctives and divisions, but there is an important ecumenical dynamic to the elevating of these four convictions above the fault lines of denominational division. Evangelicals see these four convictions as nonnegotiable elements of Christian profession and practice and therefore are willing to negotiate, or even simply to leave to each Christian community, decisions regarding all other issues of dispute, which are seen as secondary and nonessential. This transdenominationalism, therefore, is the fifth evangelical quality to round out our list.[3]

So what? That was then, this is now, and tomorrow will be yet another new context. Why should the convictions of two hundred years ago guide us in contemporary theology? Indeed, these convictions might have been helpful then, as they are today, for providing a basis for cooperative evangelistic ministry. But how useful are they theologically?

Bold and exciting it would be, indeed, to call all Christian theologians to adopt evangelical principles. I shall aim, however, at a more modest objective: to encourage evangelical theologians—that is, theologians who already take these five principles seriously for their Christian identity—to be guided by these convictions in their theological work. And as fellow Christians watch evangelicals doing so, one might entertain the hope that such Christians will find it sufficiently interesting and (more important by far) edifying so as to learn what they can from it, even as we evangelicals already are learning from them.

Evangelical Convictions and Evangelical Theology

Christ and Salvation

Evangelical theology ought to focus on Jesus Christ both epistemologically and substantively. Thus, evangelical theology ought to be both Christological and Christocentric.

In the epistemological sense, evangelicals traditionally have interpreted the Bible and gone on to construct theology primarily in the light of the revelation of God in Christ. Historical-critical exegesis of the Old Testament properly considers the process by which God's revelation of himself and his work on earth emerges in human, and particularly in Israelite, history. But evangelicals unapologetically move not only forward from the beginning to the end of so-called progressive revelation in the Old Testament but also backward from the New Testament to

3. Evangelical statesman John R. W. Stott demonstrates this quality vividly in the conclusion to his *Evangelical Truth: A Personal Plea for Unity, Integrity, and Faithfulness* (Downers Grove, Ill.: InterVarsity, 1999), 115–19.

see the Old Testament illuminated in the light of God's definitive revelation in Jesus. Similarly, as evangelicals encounter later developments in Christian thought and practice—whether the formulation of the doctrine of God as Trinity, or the understanding of the status and role of Mary and the saints, or the direction of Christian mission in the world—they properly, even reflexively, refer back always to what God has revealed of himself during the earthly career of Jesus of Nazareth.

In the substantive sense, evangelical theology views Christ as the center of God's story—the most important thing God has ever done or said. The person and work of Christ do not merely crown God's work of revelation and redemption as a sort of splendid ornament or even as the best example of God's activity in the world. The person and work of Christ constitute the defining chapter of the whole narrative, the hinge of history, the basis upon which everything else in creation makes sense.

One might think that a religion that is content to be called "Christianity" would not need evangelicals (or any others) to champion the importance of a "Christ-ian" focus to its theology. Yet in contemporary theology, as in the history of Christian thought, theologians have called theology away from its Christological and Christocentric focus.

A couple of decades ago, James Gustafson wrote his well-known ethics that calls for a "theocentric" perspective, stating straightforwardly in the title what most liberal theology has taught since Friedrich Schleiermacher—himself perhaps the first and last liberal to see the Redeemer as essential, and not just helpful, in salvation history.[4]

Process theology interprets the world through the scheme of A. N. Whitehead and his theological epigones, not through any important Christological lens. And the "salvation history" celebrated by process theology has no central role for Jesus to play. His witness to the truth of God and his example to his followers in realizing that truth constitute a considerable gift to humanity. But the actual scheme of God "luring" the world to its high-

4. James M. Gustafson, *Ethics from a Theocentric Perspective* (Chicago: University of Chicago Press, 1983); cf. Friedrich D. E. Schleiermacher, *The Christian Faith,* English translation of the 2d German ed., ed. H. R. Mackintosh and J. S. Stewart (Philadelphia: Fortress, 1928).

est end does not in any important sense *require* the career of Jesus of Nazareth, as the orthodox gospel does.[5]

It is this reduction of the importance of Jesus that, not coincidentally, links liberals such as Gustafson and process theologians such as John Cobb to a third form of contemporary Christian thought that also is determinedly non-Christological and non-Christocentric, namely, pluralism in the encounter with world religions. In the pluralism espoused by John Hick, Wilfred Cantwell Smith, Hans Küng, and many others, Jesus is one prophet among many, an admirable man who gestured instructively toward Ultimate Reality and provided a model for relating appropriately to that reality—just as Lao Tzu, Moses, Confucius, Krishna, Zoroaster, Gautama Buddha, and Muhammad did. Evangelical theology rightly maintains the "scandal of particularity" in this conversation, even as evangelicals themselves debate just how best to understand the work of Christ with regard to non-Christians and the relationship between the Christian faith and other faiths.[6]

Liberal theology of various stripes is not the only sort of theology needing correction from an evangelical focus on Christ, particularly in his cross and resurrection. Recently, evangelical theologians have encountered, and some have embraced, Orthodox theology—perhaps epitomized best in John Zizioulas's work.[7] There is much in both Orthodoxy's piety and theology to complement and even correct Roman Catho-

5. John B. Cobb, Jr., and David Ray Griffin, *Process Theology: An Introductory Exposition* (Philadelphia: Westminster, 1976).

6. Sir Norman Anderson, *Christianity and World Religions: The Challenge of Pluralism* (1970; reprint, Leicester/Downers Grove, Ill.: InterVarsity, 1980); Harold A. Netland, *Dissonant Voices: Religious Pluralism and the Question of Truth* (Grand Rapids: Eerdmans, 1991); Clark H. Pinnock, *A Wideness in God's Mercy: The Finality of Jesus Christ in a World of Religions* (Grand Rapids: Zondervan, 1992); John Sanders, *No Other Name: An Investigation into the Destiny of the Unevangelized* (Grand Rapids: Eerdmans, 1992); Gerald D. McDermott, *Can Evangelicals Learn from the Buddha?* (Downers Grove, Ill.: InterVarsity, 2000); and John G. Stackhouse, Jr., ed., *No Other Gods before Me? Evangelicals Encounter the World's Religions* (Grand Rapids: Baker, 2001).

7. For examples, see John Zizioulas, *Being as Communion: Studies in Personhood and the Church* (New York: St. Vladimir's Seminary Press, 1997); cf. John Meyendorff, *Byzantine Theology: Historical Trends and Doctrinal Themes*, 2d ed. (1974; reprint, New York: Fordham University Press, 1979).

lic and Protestant Christianity. But evangelicals who appreciate their tradition's emphasis on the cross and resurrection of
Jesus, and see such an emphasis as emergent from the New
Testament itself, will be cautious about a too hasty and too enthusiastic embrace of a theological tradition that does not
share this emphasis.

Indeed, non-Orthodox Christians have long been chary of Orthodoxy's focus on ontological categories of divinity and humanity, eternal and temporal, spirit and matter, when it comes to salvation. In the light of these concerns (which doubtless reflect
Orthodoxy's cultural cradle in the Hellenistic East), Orthodoxy
focuses more on the incarnation itself as the basis of salvation—
as God bridges the various ontic divides—and the impartation of
God's divine nature to the human soul as the central mechanism
of this salvation. However much Catholic and Protestant Christians can profit from such a theological model (and I believe we
can profit a great deal), evangelicals do well not to throw over
their model in their excitement over the riches of the Eastern traditions. Instead, evangelicals ought to recognize that Orthodoxy's model—Christ-centered as it is, in its way—also does not
fully account for the biblical portrait of Christ.

Within evangelical theology itself, finally, a Christological
and Christocentric reminder perhaps needs to be issued to
those who currently pursue trinitarianism as a sort of key to
unlock a wide range of theological puzzles. We can learn
about the one true God, yes, from Old Testament revelation
that only hints at God's trinitarian nature, but we know what
we know about the Trinity per se mostly because of God's revelation in Christ. It was, after all, the disciples' encounter with
Christ that led to their worship of him and conceptualizing of
him as the divine Lord—thus leading to a binitarian understanding of God that became trinitarian only as Christian
thought matured (indeed, one would say, only as the Holy
Spirit himself guided the church to this insight).[8] And the Holy
Spirit remains—despite some impressive expositions by evangelicals of late—a relatively minor, shadowy figure in the New
Testament compared with the center stage, fully lit person of

8. Larry W. Hurtado, *One God, One Lord: Early Christian Devotion and Ancient Jewish Monotheism* (Philadelphia: Fortress, 1988).

Jesus.[9] For all we know, to put the point more provocatively than it perhaps should be put, God might actually be "quadritarian"—or more complex still. Christian theology, after all, has inferred the triune nature of God from what we see in God's revelation in Christ.

Of course evangelicals should be trinitarian (for we have no evidence that God is more than a trinity and lots of evidence that he is), and of course we should plumb what depths we can of God's revelation of himself as triune in order to know and enjoy and serve him best. My concern here is simply to emphasize that we evangelicals ought to maintain our Christological approach and Christocentric emphasis in all doctrine, including the doctrine of God. This tradition will keep us from presuming to know more about, and emphasizing more than we should about, the Holy Spirit, or God the Father, or the Triune God in Godself. God the Holy Spirit points us to Christ, and Christ is the one who shows us God the Father.

The Bible

Evangelicals have always been "Bible people." Evangelicalism typically has championed excellent preaching, personal Bible study, general biblical literacy—all in the name of the unique authority of the Bible for our belief and practice. Evangelicals have symbolized this regard for the Bible typically by erecting impressive pulpits in the center of church platforms, by lionizing great preachers, and by observing rituals of everyday piety, such as never letting a Bible rest on the floor or be covered by another book.

Indeed, among the criticisms most frequently leveled against evangelicals is that we are *too* focused on the Bible at the expense of not taking other God-given theological resources as seriously as we should, whether tradition, reason, or experience. A similar criticism runs that evangelicals are simplistic in their interpretation of the Bible and use of it in theology—seeing the Bible as a two-dimensional plane of proof-texts that can be ap-

9. Gordon D. Fee, *God's Empowering Presence: The Holy Spirit in the Letters of Paul* (Peabody, Mass.: Hendrickson, 1994); and Clark H. Pinnock, *Flame of Love: A Theology of the Holy Spirit* (Downers Grove, Ill.: InterVarsity, 1996).

plied directly to matters of doctrine or ethics without recognizing the realities of progressive revelation, genre differences, and other important qualifications of the "voice" of the Bible. These attitudes combine to form a syndrome that places the text of the Bible at the center of evangelical life and in fact displaces the Holy Spirit's role as primary teacher, thus amounting to a bibliolatry.

Evangelical theologians, aided especially by the findings of our colleagues in the historical study of evangelicalism, can wince and agree with many aspects of these charges.[10] In our embarrassment over our overuse, misuse, and abuse of the Bible, however, we might yield to the temptation to surrender the kernel in the midst of so much husk. That kernel remains the unique and supreme authority of the Bible as both itself the Word of God written and as an unequaled tool in the hands of the Spirit of God to render God's Word to us today.

To be sure, the renewed interest in the historical theology of the church and the postmodern critique of epistemology have combined to warn contemporary evangelical theologians not to confuse any particular interpretation of the Bible with the Bible itself. The Bible is God's Word written, but our interpretations of it are not. And our interpretations of the Bible may well need to be adjusted in the light of our interpretations of God's other means of revelation, whether science, history, tradition, spiritual experience, and so on—just as, nonetheless, our interpretations of those phenomena also ought to be in respectful dialogue with our understanding of Scripture. Indeed, truly evangelical thinking about any subject will always privilege scriptural interpretation and never willfully contradict what the Scripture at least *seems* to say—however much tension we must live with while we try to sort out apparent contradictions.[11]

Our own generation has been blessed by some first-rate wrestling with matters of the nature of the Bible, its authority,

10. Mark A. Noll, *Between Faith and Criticism: Evangelicals, Scholarship, and the Bible in America* (San Francisco: Harper & Row, 1986).

11. For quite different but complementary statements of this point, see Donald A. D. Thorsen, *The Wesleyan Quadrilateral: Scripture, Tradition, Reason, and Experience as a Model of Evangelical Theology* (Grand Rapids: Zondervan, 1990); and Nicholas Wolterstorff, *Reason within the Bounds of Religion*, rev. ed. (1976; reprint, Grand Rapids: Eerdmans, 1979).

its interpretation, and its application to our lives: Books by Anthony Thiselton, Kevin Vanhoozer, Nicholas Wolterstorff, and Tom Wright shine among other luminaries in a constellation of scholarship.[12] No one supposes, however, that we have sorted out all of the pertinent issues.

Indeed, few have ventured to respond to postmodernism with a theology that takes it seriously from the inside and responds to it with biblical truth: Richard Middleton and Brian Walsh's pioneering *Truth Is Stranger than It Used to Be* is a lonely effort in this vein.[13] Evangelicalism has yet to produce a substantial theology written from a feminist perspective. On this score, we continue to spend our limited theological resources arguing about, among other things, whether women can be theologians at all. But where is the theology—or even the sustained biblical study as resource for such theology— that starts with evangelical premises and pays attention to gender, to power, to women, and to other subjects overlooked by male-dominated theology, and in modes unexplored by such theology heretofore? And formal evangelical theology written from the perspective of the Third World is relayed to us mostly by informed Americans (such as William Dyrness) and expatriates (such as Lamin Sanneh)—even as informal theology, especially in Pentecostal and charismatic modes from Argentina and Korea, flows powerfully into "sending" countries such as ours.[14]

12. See several successive books by Anthony C. Thiselton, beginning with *The Two Horizons: New Testament Hermeneutics and Philosophical Description* (Grand Rapids: Eerdmans, 1980); Kevin J. Vanhoozer, *Is There a Meaning in This Text? The Bible, the Reader, and the Morality of Literary Knowledge* (Grand Rapids: Zondervan, 1998); Nicholas Wolterstorff, *Divine Discourse: Philosophical Reflections on the Claim That God Speaks* (Cambridge: Cambridge University Press, 1995); and the series begun by N. T. Wright with *The New Testament and the People of God* (Minneapolis: Fortress, 1992).

13. J. Richard Middleton and Brian J. Walsh, *Truth Is Stranger than It Used to Be: Biblical Faith in a Postmodern Age* (Downers Grove, Ill.: InterVarsity, 1995).

14. Lamin Sanneh, *Translating the Message: The Missionary Impact on Culture* (Maryknoll, N.Y.: Orbis, 1994); and William A. Dyrness, *Learning about Theology from the Third World* (Grand Rapids: Zondervan, 1990). See also William A. Dyrness, gen. ed., *Emerging Voices in Global Christian Theology* (Grand Rapids: Zondervan, 1994).

Evangelical respect for the Bible continues, however, to be needed in theology today. Resistance to the full affirmation of homosexuality—especially in the face of the collapse of the psychological and psychiatric community's recognition of its pathology—can be justified only on the basis of something like an evangelical Scripture principle. Anything short of a clear divine word can be dismissed as mere human convention or invention and thus simply "homophobic." What is true of this particular debate is true of other ethical debates as well: Discussion of the legitimacy of war, capital punishment, care for the poor, and so on is crucially shaped in each case by whether we believe we have authoritative guidance from God in Scripture.

Evangelicals properly distance themselves from a liberal methodology that feels "free" to ignore, and even contradict, express teachings of Scripture in the name of the putative superiority of current opinion. And evangelicals continue properly to wonder just how "postliberal" postliberals really are in this respect. Do they stand under the authority of the Bible—even the awkward parts, even the parts that seem sexist, or fantastic, or wrong—or are they still working with too much liberal freedom?[15]

A sound allegiance to the authority of the Bible, furthermore, speaks to at least three dangerous trends within evangelicalism itself. One trend has evangelicals engaged in theological speculation, particularly associated with the doctrine of the Trinity, in ways that would be profitably chastened by a closer tethering to the scriptural text. Indeed, it is becoming common to hear an evangelical theologian simply make the following syllogistic move without recourse to Scripture itself: "God, the Holy Trinity, is X; we are created in God's image; therefore, we are X."[16] Martin Luther and John Calvin, who wrote a great deal about

15. See the engagement of evangelicals and postliberals on some of these questions in Timothy R. Phillips and Dennis L. Okholm, eds., *The Nature of Confession: Evangelicals and Postliberals in Conversation* (Downers Grove, Ill.: InterVarsity, 1996); see also William C. Placher's candid recognition of precisely this issue in *Narratives of a Vulnerable God: Christ, Theology, and Scripture* (Louisville: Westminster John Knox, 1994), 126–27.

16. Colin Gunton is arguably the most important theologian of this type. His writing honestly attests at times to his own ambivalence about using the doctrine of the Trinity as a kind of "control" or "way into" other theological issues. When it comes to the nature of the church, for instance, he acknowledges that "different theologies of the Trinity generate correspondingly different ec-

God, nonetheless would chide us for repeating the scholastic mistake of presuming to venture much beyond the scriptural text into the abyss of Godself.[17]

A second dangerous trend is heading in the other direction, toward a traditionalism, even a credalism, that is satisfied that God has broken forth all the light from his holy Word that he is ever going to break. If the previous danger is that of speculation, we now encounter the danger of formalism. It arises in evangelicalism nowadays with certain devotees of certain brands of Reformed orthodoxy, often dubbed the "Truly Reformed" by those who have felt the sting of their criticism. These warriors not only claim to speak authoritatively and univocally for what is in fact a multistranded Reformed tradition but then presume to speak for all evangelicals (as in the Alliance of Confessing Evangelicals).[18]

Evangelical allegiance to the Bible would instead take all of us to the place of John Calvin, who revised his own summary of doctrine (the *Institutes of the Christian Religion*) several times—without, to my knowledge, ever claiming infallibility for it. Or perhaps to the place of Martin Luther, who never felt it urgent to systematize his theology. Or to Jonathan Edwards and John

---

clesiologies" (Colin E. Gunton, *The Promise of Trinitarian Theology* [Edinburgh: T & T Clark, 1991], 74; see also Miroslav Volf, *After Our Likeness: The Church as the Image of the Trinity* [Grand Rapids: Eerdmans, 1998], especially 214–20). Indeed, when it comes to the particular question of gender in the church, egalitarians (such as Gunton) appeal to the "perichoretic dance" of the Trinity, while hierarchalists appeal to the eternal subordination of the Son to the Father (e.g., Michael Harper, *Equal and Different: Male and Female in the Church and Family* [London: Hodder & Stoughton, 1997], 153–63). Space here does not permit an adequate discussion of this issue. But one perhaps can fairly raise the question of just how truly illuminative and directive the mystery of the Trinity can be in this respect, and how much we should instead look at more explicit biblical guidance in considering this or that theological issue. (For a recent attempt to set out a trinitarian guide to hermeneutics from a conservative Reformed American point of view, see Vern S. Poythress, *God-Centered Biblical Interpretation* [Phillipsburg, N.J.: Presbyterian & Reformed, 1999].)

17. See B. A. Gerrish, "'To the Unknown God': Luther and Calvin on the Hiddenness of God," in *The Old Protestantism and the New* (Chicago: University of Chicago Press; Edinburgh: T & T Clark, 1982), 131–49.

18. So several books by David F. Wells beginning with *No Place for Truth, or, Whatever Happened to Evangelical Theology?* (Grand Rapids: Eerdmans, 1993); for the ACE, see www.AllianceNet.org.

Wesley, who wrote much theology in their different ways but always to meet the needs of their contemporaries, not presuming to speak for generations past or to generations in the future. The Bible, they each recognized, was inexhaustibly rich, complicated, and mysterious—just as one would expect from a divine Author.

The "Truly Reformed" formalists are joined, of course, by those other credalists who are willing to put their own tradition's statements of faith, whether the Canons and Decrees of the Council of Trent, the Canons of Dort, the Westminster Confession, the Formula of Concord, the Thirty-Nine Articles, or the Lausanne Covenant, above any fresh reading of Scripture. Such doctrinaire theologians parallel those Christians who rigorously defend traditional liturgies (whether traditional Anglican, traditional Mennonite, or traditional Pentecostal!), traditional hierarchies (whether ecclesiastical or domestic), or traditional devotional practices (whether saying a rosary or having a "daily quiet time") without continual openness to scriptural investigation to "see if these things be true" (Acts 17:11). Evangelical biblicism at its best, then, is not only a conservative force but also a radical dynamic. It frees theology from automatic conformity to any such human approximations of God's truth—wonderful gifts to the church as many of these traditions may be.

A third danger is the danger of mysticism, of spiritual experience trumping all other claims to knowledge. Evangelicalism has always gloried in spiritual experience. One of its chief characteristics, I am in fact arguing, is its emphasis on personal conversion. "You ask me how I know he lives," evangelicals still like to sing, "he lives within my heart." And recent Christian work in epistemology (one thinks of William Alston especially) has been reclaiming spiritual experience as cognitively important, not merely personally moving.[19]

The worthiness of spiritual experience as a theological resource is not in question here, however. My question concerns

19. William P. Alston, *Perceiving God: The Epistemology of Religious Experience* (Ithaca, N.Y./London: Cornell University Press, 1991); cf. the unusual argument in Phillip H. Wiebe, *Visions of Jesus: Direct Encounters from the New Testament to Today* (New York/Oxford: Oxford University Press, 1997).

mysticism as a cognitive style. "I believe God is saying . . ." can function dangerously as "Thus saith the Lord . . ." unless everyone agrees to place priority on God's written Word as supreme guide to those who exercise discernment over such prophecy. Failure to truly give such priority to the Bible is at the root of many oddities in contemporary mystical movements, whether charismatic (as in the Toronto Blessing) or devotees of particular mystical writers (such as Madame Guyon or Thomas Merton).[20] And such extremes point to the importance for evangelical theology of keeping together in right balance all five of these evangelical convictions.

One of the earliest practitioners of historical or "higher" criticism of the Bible was the zealous Roman Catholic Roger Simon. His agenda in the face of the rise of Protestantism was transparent: to so undermine the Bible's authority that any sensible and devout Christian would flee from the broken reed of *sola scriptura* to the strong, wise guidance of Mother Church. In our own day, ironically, the Jesus Seminar and certain other higher critics seek to undermine the Bible's authority in order to encourage a move in the opposite direction, toward a religious pluralism that glorifies no one particular religion or leader or scripture as divinely authoritative. Centuries ago, Roger Simon recognized the crucial importance of a "high" doctrine of Scripture. So today does Robert Funk. Evangelicals must not forget it.

Conversion

Princeton Seminary's Ellen Charry has been bringing a widely noted message to academic theology of late. In her book, *By the Renewing of Your Minds,* she reminds us that once upon a time—indeed, in most times until our own—Christians pursued theology in the cause of spiritual transformation.[21] Theology, that is, was no mere intellectual exercise, let alone a full-time profession that even unbelievers could undertake (*pace*

---

20. James A. Beverley, *Holy Laughter and the Toronto Blessing: An Investigative Report* (Grand Rapids: Zondervan, 1995); I know of no scholarly study of the widespread evangelical interest in Madame Guyon, Thomas Merton, and other non-evangelical mystics.

21. Ellen T. Charry, *By the Renewing of Your Minds: The Pastoral Function of Christian Doctrine* (New York/Oxford: Oxford University Press, 1999).

Paul Tillich and David Tracy).[22] Theology always served the fundamental Christian concern for conversion.

When Professor Charry graced our theology conference at Regent College in 1998, however, she found (to her express delight) that she was bringing coals to Newcastle. For all of evangelicalism's many faults, both theological and spiritual, evangelicals at least have kept theology and piety together as an ideal, and often as a reality as well. Theology is doxology, as J. I. Packer likes to put it, and it is properly (to borrow a phrase from Andrew Murray) an "aid to devotion." Certainly Calvin intended his "handbook" (or *Institutio*) to serve in this way. Whether one considers John Wesley or Jonathan Edwards, Charles Finney or Charles Hodge, Donald Barnhouse or Donald Bloesch, John Wimber or John Stott, evangelicals characteristically view theology as fundamentally concerned with the new birth and the subsequent life of discipleship.

Beyond the academic theology indicted by Charry, some other forms of contemporary theology, particularly those with a clear political focus, also have neglected the spiritual dimension of the Christian message. If we turn to feminist theology, we find that some exponents—not all of them, of course—preoccupy themselves with secular matters: who occupies which position in the ecclesiastical hierarchy or domestic economy, and more general questions of how women are to function and be treated in a just society. Some forms of liberation theology—again, not all of them—similarly have been criticized for focusing on the amelioration of economic and social oppression to the exclusion of spiritual deliverance.

In such programs of social concern, one can sympathize with activists who fear that any promise of "pie in the sky by and by" will cut the nerve of the political revolutions they see to be mandated by Christian compassion and justice. They hear Marx's warning about religion's narcotic powers, and they also are inspired by the New Testament, which denounces those who intone good wishes for the needy without lifting a finger to help them (James 2:16).

22. For Tracy, following Tillich, see David Tracy, *Blessed Rage for Order: The New Pluralism in Theology* (Minneapolis: Winston/Seabury, 1975), especially 57 n. 3.

Still, an evangelical will prefer the wholistic agenda of a Gustavo Gutiérrez, and particularly of our own Ron Sider.[23] These theologians have established irreproachable records of advocacy for the needy while steadfastly proclaiming the "whole counsel of God." This counsel demands care for the poor that includes the good news of God's offer of conversion in Christ as the heart of his plan to restore all of creation to shalom—indeed, his plan of cosmic conversion.[24]

Evangelical theologians, furthermore, will beware of the lure of strictly academic theology. To be sure, it seems rather odd to warn evangelicals of excessive intellectualism: The "scandal of the evangelical mind" seems not to lie in overindulgence in arcana.[25]

But as evangelicals continue to graduate from prestigious research universities and enter the professional guilds of the Society for Biblical Literature, American Academy of Religion, and other such high-altitude organizations, we do well to maintain the life-giving linkage between the science of theology and the *scientia* that begins with the "fear of the LORD," the vital connection of head, heart, and hands that characterized so many of our evangelical forebears.

Mission

Therefore, in the light of this our faith and our resolve, we enter into a solemn covenant with God and with each other, to pray, to plan and to work together for the evangelization of the whole world. We call upon others to join us. May God help us by his grace and for his glory to be faithful to this our covenant! Amen, Alleluia![26]

Thus ends the Lausanne Covenant (1974), perhaps the definitive statement of international evangelical commitment in the

23. Gustavo Gutiérrez, *A Theology of Liberation: History, Politics, and Salvation*, rev. ed., trans. Caridad Inda and John Eagleson (Maryknoll, N.Y.: Orbis, 1988); and Ronald J. Sider, *Living like Jesus: Eleven Essentials for Growing a Genuine Faith* (Grand Rapids: Baker, 1999).

24. So William A. Dyrness, *The Earth Is God's: A Theology of American Culture* (Maryknoll, N.Y.: Orbis, 1997); and Nicholas Wolterstorff, *Until Justice and Peace Embrace* (Grand Rapids: Eerdmans, 1983).

25. Mark A. Noll, *The Scandal of the Evangelical Mind* (Grand Rapids: Eerdmans, 1994).

26. Lausanne Covenant, 1974. Online: http://www.lausanne.org/statements/covenant.html.

twentieth century. The Covenant places mission, and particularly evangelistic mission, at the center of the church's role in the world. It recognizes worship, compassionate ministry of various sorts, and the edification of the church as key responsibilities for all Christians. But it affirms that evangelism is the central call of God on the church in this epoch.

Not all evangelicals—and certainly not all Christians—endorse this priority.[27] Some take their cues from what they read in other traditions, notably Roman Catholic or Orthodox Christianity, and declare worship to be the church's main task, now and ever. Others see the church's primary responsibility to lie in care for the needy, and while such service will involve spiritual counsel at times, such counsel is only a part of a full-orbed representation of God's purposes in the world. And many evangelicals act as if the kingdom of God consists entirely of the steady expansion of congregations, church buildings, and parachurch agencies.

Even if for the sake of argument, however, we leave aside the knotty question of just which of the good things Lausanne says the church is to do deserves priority, evangelicals cannot be evangelicals without endorsing the importance of evangelism. And even this less controversial affirmation—which, one might think, would be endorsed by every Christian—sets evangelical theology over against some trends in contemporary Christian thought.

For one thing, it keeps evangelical theology from falling into the respective ditches of liberal and postliberal theology. The liberal tendency is to echo the culture—or, at least, to echo certain elites in that culture. This liberal "evangelism," perhaps exemplified best today in the proselytizing efforts of the Jesus Seminar, John Spong, and Hans Küng, says very little to the culture that the culture is not already saying. Indeed, its fundamental message seems to be directed not toward the culture at all but to traditional Christians in the kerygmatic formulation of Bishop Spong, "Change or die!"[28]

27. It is more than a little ironic that just as some evangelicals are disputing the priority of evangelism, some mainline and Anabaptist Protestants are reaffirming it. See Darrell L. Guder, ed., *Missional Church: A Vision for the Sending of the Church in North America* (Grand Rapids: Eerdmans, 1998).

28. John Shelby Spong, *Why Christianity Must Change or Die: A Bishop Speaks to Believers in Exile* (San Francisco: HarperSanFrancisco, 1998).

Postliberalism, for its part, retains a commitment to the gospel as traditionally understood in many respects, but its tendency, reacting as it does to the liberalism that is its constant foil, is to sectarianism and even unintelligibility. An evangelical will fear that postliberalism's stout insistence on retaining the church's own language and subsuming the contemporary world (somehow) into the biblical world can entail (as it did for Barth) a denial of sufficient common ground with the world upon which to proclaim the faith—despite the evident cultural sophistication of scholars in this school. Apologetics, therefore, is at best an ad hoc enterprise (as Hans Frei and William Werpehowski put it) and perhaps at worst a simply dubious one (as Barth thought it was). It is not at all clear, as William Placher himself candidly puts it, how postliberals can suggest that what they themselves have found in Christianity to be true can be proclaimed as "just plain true" for everyone.[29]

And therefore evangelism becomes deeply problematic.

In fairness to the postliberals, however, the postmodern critique of knowledge does render problematic the proclamation of a universal gospel. Indeed, a cutting edge for evangelical theology today—as it is for any form of Christian theology that takes evangelism seriously—is to work out the epistemological grounds upon which we can then compose the most appropriate forms of evangelistic address to our neighbors. Analyses of some fundamental problems have been undertaken by an impressive group of scholars, ranging from sociologists such as Craig Gay and David Lyon to theologians such as Richard Middleton and Brian Walsh to philosophers such as Alvin Plantinga and Nicholas Wolterstorff.[30]

29. William C. Placher, *Unapologetic Theology: A Christian Voice in a Pluralistic Conversation* (Louisville: Westminster John Knox, 1989), 163–66.

30. Craig M. Gay, *The Way of the (Modern) World: Or, Why It's Tempting to Live as If God Doesn't Exist* (Grand Rapids: Eerdmans; Cumbria, U.K.: Paternoster; Vancouver: Regent College, 1998); David Lyon, *Postmodernity* (Minneapolis: University of Minnesota Press, 1994); Middleton and Walsh, *Truth Is Stranger than It Used to Be;* Alvin Plantinga, the three-volume series on warrant that begins with *Warrant: The Current Debate* (New York/Oxford: Oxford University Press, 1993); and Wolterstorff, *Reason;* and *Divine Discourse.*

What have yet to emerge clearly are a posture and a rhetoric appropriate to evangelism in such conditions.[31] Indeed, if evangelicals are to continue to prize evangelism, then more of us must engage, and engage in, apologetics—both working out its theory for this cultural moment and actually undertaking conversation with thoughtful "others" in our culture. We must not confine, as we currently do, the great preponderance of our theological efforts to addressing either the church or the religious studies academy.

By extension, of course, it is evangelicalism's commitment not only to our neighbors but also to world evangelization that should prompt evangelical theology's investigation of perhaps the greatest theological question of our time: the plurality of the world's religions. The state of the art, alas, consists of evangelicals disputing over whether anyone who has not heard an authentic presentation of the gospel by the Holy Spirit can somehow be saved. Only elementary work, and not much of it, has been done so far toward constructing a thorough theology of religions that can explain world religions under the providence of God, and then suggest how Christian evangelism should be carried out in the light of such a theological understanding. It is a paradox, and perhaps an indictment, of evangelical theology that theological liberals have been working on this question in detail for years while evangelicals—whose missionaries continue to have the most actual contact with people of other faiths—lag conceptually far behind.

Indeed, one of the greatest scandals of evangelical theology in our time—and of academic theology in general—is the almost complete disinterest such theology has for the experience and reflection of missionaries and missiologists. Yet theologians today would do well to link the ivory tower and the mission field, to draw together *Theology Today* and the *Interna-*

31. A good beginning is made in David Clark, *Dialogical Apologetics: A Person-Centered Approach to Christian Defense* (Grand Rapids: Baker, 1993). For examples of a change in tone from the common evidentialist and rationalist forms of evangelical apologetics, see Kelly James Clark, *When Faith Is Not Enough* (Grand Rapids/Cambridge, U.K.: Eerdmans, 1997); Thomas V. Morris, *Making Sense of It All: Pascal and the Meaning of Life* (Grand Rapids: Eerdmans, 1992); and my *Can God Be Trusted? Faith and the Challenge of Evil* (New York/Oxford: Oxford University Press, 1998). See also my *Humble Apologetics: Defending the Faith Today* (New York/Oxford: Oxford University Press, 2002).

tional Bulletin of Missionary Research. What historian David Bebbington calls the "activistic" quality of evangelicalism has often militated against the sedentary work of theology, as action takes precedence over reflection. But if one looks at the theology written by Paul the missionary in the New Testament; the work of the early Greek apologists; Thomas Aquinas's missionary handbook, the *Summa Contra Gentiles;* or the musings of Jonathan Edwards on the missionary frontier of colonial Massachusetts, one sees that the evangelistic impulse has galvanized Christian theology many times, and wonderfully, throughout church history. Evangelical theologians should joyfully seek its energy today.

Transdenominationalism

Evangelicalism's elevation of the previous four concerns above all others has allowed evangelicals to band together on a variety of Christian projects: relief and development, publishing and broadcasting, education from preschool to graduate school, music, and evangelism both domestic and international, among many others.

When it comes to theology, this transdenominational openness has also positioned evangelicals to engage in dialogue with Roman Catholics, postliberals, and the Eastern Orthodox.[32]

Evangelicals also have increasingly contributed to mainline theological inquiry, notably in the pages of both academic journals and middlebrow periodicals such as *Theology Today* and the *Christian Century.* Each of these is a dramatic development when viewed from the perspective of just a generation or two ago, whether one's perspective is British, American, or Canadian.

But one can ask for more—and less. For more, we could ask that evangelicals capitalize on their transdenominationalism beyond affirming their lowest common denominator of theol-

32. For the "Evangelicals and Catholics Together" document and evangelical commentary, see *Christianity Today* 41 (8 December 1997): 34; or www2.chris tianity.net/ct/7TE/7TE034.html. For evangelicals and postliberals, see Phillips and Okholm, *Nature of Confession.* For an example of evangelical-Orthodox theological exchange, see the articles by J. I. Packer and Bradley Nassif in *Crux* 32 (September 1996): 12–32; see also the magazine *Touchstone,* which brings together certain conservatives of Catholic, Protestant, and Orthodox traditions.

ogy or acknowledging respectfully their various differences (so the genre of books that offer "four views" on this or that area of disagreement). Could evangelicals profitably seek to read one another, as well as reading liberals of various stripes, postliberals, Catholics, and others, in order to refine their own views precisely on the secondary, but still important, matters on which evangelicals disagree?

It seems to me that an evangelical transdenominationalism might dispose an evangelical Calvinist toward considering more seriously than he might the merits of Arminian or Pentecostal theology since such a Calvinist already recognizes and affirms his Arminian brother or Pentecostal sister as not only a fellow Christian but also a fellow evangelical. Mennonites are sometimes read with profit by evangelicals—John Howard Yoder is exhibit A—but do Anabaptist evangelicals read other evangelicals in order to refine (I do not say "desert") their outlook? Such a perspective—that starts from a given tradition but is inclined to appreciate, not merely guard against, other evangelical traditions—might lift us beyond inherited impasses and draw on fresh light regarding perennial mysteries such as original sin, the relation of human will and divine providence, and the nature and scope of the atonement.

Evangelicals hold conferences to learn from one another regarding worship, preaching, church growth, social action, and other areas of joint concern. Will we support conferences that also bring together different viewpoints on gender, salvation, polity, the fate of the unevangelized, God's redemption of creation, and so on that help each of us become at least better versions of ourselves? Wheaton College's theology conference is a good step in this direction, and I hope Regent's conference will be another. When the *Journal of the Evangelical Theological Society* has avoided mere diatribes to concentrate on constructive work, it has offered useful fruit. In this regard, I believe that our British counterparts have much to show us, particularly in the ongoing example of the Tyndale Fellowship and the journal *Themelios*—which regretfully have no exact parallels in either Canada or the United States, as they have fostered evangelical theological excellence for more than a generation.[33]

33. For an appreciative American account, see Noll, *Between Faith and Criticism*, chap. 4 and passim.

We can also ask for less, however. We can ask for less arrogance and energy devoted to sorting out who are the true evangelicals and who are the pretenders, deviants, or apostates.[34] We can ask for definitions of evangelicalism that are truly as broad as historic evangelicalism has been and then move on to the interesting and important work that theology has to do in our time. Indeed, as a Canadian with some familiarity with the American scene, I wonder if British and Canadian evangelicals have less inclination to specify sharp boundaries of authentic evangelicalism, not because we are morally or spiritually or intellectually superior to our American cousins, but because we simply cannot afford the luxury of continual heresy hunting and the division that it produces. Indeed, the logic of my argument is that such intra-evangelical wars are actually anti-evangelical.[35]

A robust transdenominationalism, finally, should promote respect for difference in secondary matters and devotion to the central importance of Jesus Christ and his gospel. Such an attitude fosters related theological virtues of zeal tempered by reserve, of confidence qualified by humility. Evangelicalism at its best keeps these pairs in play and, by God's grace, in balance.

Conclusion

Evangelical theology has profited in the past as it has attended to the voices of other Christians and, indeed, people of other faiths and philosophies. Evangelical theology, according to the sketch I have set out here, does not and cannot answer every question and solve every problem. Still, I have found it to be a good stance from which to consider theological challenges.

34. At this particular juncture, I have deliberately avoided the scholarly convention of providing examples of the genre in question precisely because I do not want to fight fire with fire, denunciation with denunciation. Readers who are not already familiar with such diatribes can count themselves blessed.

35. Thus, when Gary Dorrien suggests that evangelicalism "has been poorly suited to affirm pluralism of any kind" and that "the evangelical impulse is to insist that only one religious tradition can be true," he overlooks the transdenominational dimension of evangelical conviction and focuses instead on the dogmatic and sectarian dimensions only (*The Remaking of Evangelical Theology* [Louisville: Westminster John Knox, 1998], 3).

I see no compelling reason to abandon it for another. I recommend it to theologians of other stripes as a resource well worth exploring for their own enrichment. Most centrally, I encourage my fellow evangelical theologians to engage unapologetically in theology from this perspective and to maintain this historic balancing of evangelical convictions as they do.

11

Speaking in Tongues

Communicating the Gospel Today

When the day of Pentecost had come, they were all together in one place. And suddenly from heaven there came a sound like the rush of a violent wind, and it filled the entire house where they were sitting. Divided tongues, as of fire, appeared among them, and a tongue rested on each of them. All of them were filled with the Holy Spirit and began to speak in other languages, as the Spirit gave them ability.

Now there were devout Jews from every nation under heaven living in Jerusalem. And at this sound the crowd gathered and was bewildered, because each one heard them speaking in the native language of each. Amazed and astonished, they asked, "Are not all these who are speaking Galileans? And how is it that we hear, each of us, in our own native language? Parthians, Medes, Elamites, and residents of Mesopotamia, Judea and Cappadocia, Pontus and Asia, Phrygia and Pamphylia, Egypt and the parts of Libya belonging to Cyrene, and visitors from Rome, both Jews and proselytes, Cretans and Arabs—in our own languages we hear them speaking about God's deeds of power." All were amazed and perplexed, saying to one another, "What does this mean?" But others sneered and said, "They are filled with new wine."

Acts 2:1–13 NRSV

It is fundamental to the Christian religion that its members proclaim the gospel to all people with the intention that some, at least, of those who hear will become disciples. Christianity, that is, joins with Islam and Buddhism as one of the world's great missionary religions.

Evangelical Christians in particular are enthusiastic about communication with others. Sometimes, to be sure, zeal has run ahead of other virtues, such as humility and gentleness. Thus, evangelical testimony has been stereotyped, not entirely unfairly, as argumentative, dogmatic, and relentless.

For all of these faults of impoliteness or even arrogance, however, evangelicals have often failed at another fundamental level: Sometimes our witness has been, in a word, unintelligible. Our friends, family, coworkers, and fellow students—whom for this discussion we will call "our neighbors," the ones nearby— have not responded to our message because they simply have not understood it. Yes, resistance to the gospel can stem from a moral refusal to consent to the truth, but much of our neighbors' misunderstanding, I submit, has been our fault—and a fault that can be remedied.

The Need to Translate

Evangelical failures in evangelism—and the failures of other Christians as well—have stemmed in large part from two related failures that can be described as *linguistic*. We have not articulated the gospel clearly and powerfully in our "native language" of Christian tradition, and we have not translated the gospel clearly and powerfully into the languages of our neighbors. Thus, we have failed to do what the apostolic church did so well in the opening Bible passage: to speak in tongues in a way that both edifies the church and informs our society in terms it understands.

Christian proclamation in North America today—by which I mean "cultural" North America of Canada and the United States—faces at least two major cultural, and thus linguistic, impediments. (These impediments are not confined to North America, of course, but are characteristic of several other modern societies.) I want to explain how I see these two impediments and then suggest how Christians can overcome them, at least sometimes and in part, in our efforts to acquaint our neighbors with the good news that means so much to us.

Widespread Ignorance of the Christian Religion

More than a decade ago, Canadian sociologist Reginald Bibby demonstrated what many of us would have guessed from personal experience: Canadians generally identify themselves as Christians, but many practice only a little, and understand even less, of the historic Christian religion. Numbers compiled by George Gallup, Jr., and his associates do not make the American case look much brighter.[1]

At least two types of these data point to the ignorance that is typical of most North Americans regarding even the fundamentals of the Christian faith. One set describes the lack of basic Bible knowledge among Canadians. Bibby's team found in 1985 that only half of their sample knew that Elijah, Ezekiel, and Jeremiah were Old Testament prophets and that Paul was not. Only one-quarter recognized that Leviticus and Deuteronomy were *not* prophets. As for the New Testament, Bibby's project found that fewer than three out of five could identify the disciple who denied Jesus three times, while one out of five confidently gave the wrong answer. The remainder admitted ignorance. It is unlikely that these numbers have improved in the following two decades.

Beyond Bible facts, let's also consider fundamental ideas. Any introduction to the Christian religion must attempt to explain doctrines such as the incarnation, the Trinity, and atonement. Christianity is simply unintelligible without them. It is probable that most of our neighbors, then, lack a simple, correct understanding of these basic concepts. Indeed, it would be interesting to know how many Christian clergy could clearly explain them.

Bibby's second set of data pertinent to this discussion reveals that more than one-third of Canadians believe in astrology and (at least by the early 1990s) more than one-quarter testify to belief in reincarnation—while more than 80 percent, in a Canadian census taken in 1991, claimed they were Christians. Therefore, a significant chunk of the Canadian population fits into

1. Reginald W. Bibby, *Fragmented Gods: The Poverty and Potential of Religion in Canada* (Toronto: Irwin, 1987); and George Gallup, Jr., and Sarah Jones, *100 Questions and Answers: Religion in America* (Princeton, N.J.: Princeton Religion Research Center, 1989).

both camps: believing in astrology or reincarnation while identifying themselves as Christians. These neighbors apparently know so little of the Christian faith that they see no contradiction in espousing elements of mutually exclusive systems of belief.

Increasing Distance in Popular Ethos

If the situation was merely that of a decline in basic knowledge of the Christian religion, the churches could embark on a program of public education with the hope of remedying things in short order. But ignorance of the Christian faith in our culture is compounded by an equally fundamental problem: a growing distance between Christian ways of deciding about matters of truth and virtue and other ways of deciding about such things.

To pick an example both obvious and important, we can look at sexuality. What is sex? Is it good? If so, what is it good for, and who should enjoy it? From poll data to television shows to movies to media editorials to elementary school materials, it has been obvious since the sexual revolution of the 1960s that the simple Christian idea of sexual intercourse as holy and good if and only if practiced between a husband and a wife is a minority view. More fundamental, though, is the observation that the very way most North Americans decide about sexual issues is not Christian. Who seeks nowadays to investigate all that the Bible says about such matters so as to submit to its authority? Who listens attentively to the clergy? Who takes time to seek traditional wisdom?

These questions are truly rhetorical: We know their answers as soon as they are posed. Furthermore, questions concerning sexuality are simply a leading edge of a more fundamental agenda that is coming to greater and greater dominance in our society: personal liberty, which is to say, license.

Homosexuality is the cause de jour, but it is a curious one. Why is this issue the litmus test of proper—that is, "correct"— thinking when so few people actually engage in homosexual relations? (Alfred Kinsey's scurrilous propaganda that 10 percent of the population is homosexual has been chastened back to 2 or 3 percent, according to many experts—a proportion that itself may still be much too high.) Homosexuality has become

significant as the latest battleground in the war for sexual freedom, and that war is itself a campaign within the larger revolution in personal liberty. Premarital sex is no longer stigmatized.
Indeed, virginity is now so odd as to count as one of the few
things about which an aspiring sophisticate might nowadays
feel shame. Extramarital sex is still generally frowned upon,
but one-third of North Americans admit to having had at least
one affair, and novels featuring adultery join soap opera infi-
delity as the preferred entertainment of millions. So what is the
next obvious step in the quest for total individual freedom and
pleasure? Normalization of homosexuality.

Gay-bashing—verbally or physically—is a sin. Christians
need to condemn many kinds of discrimination against homosexual people. But Christians also need to stand against the
contemporary cultural efforts to flatly contradict basic biblical
teaching about the nature of human beings as reflected in sexual relations.

Yet what we need to recognize more fundamentally, both
within our church disputes on this matter and in society at
large, is that this cultural dispute is not fundamentally about
homosexuality but about ethical authority. Who or what is
going to say what is right or wrong? The reflexive answer from
the man on the street, the woman on the legal bench, or the
cleric in the pulpit is the same in many cases: a vulgar, shallow
liberalism that amounts merely to the bromide that the individual should be free to do what he or she likes as long as his or her
freedom does not impinge on another's.

When it comes to ultimate matters, then, many of our North
American neighbors have resorted either to a secularism that
frees one from all religious authority or to a hyper-individualistic
"religion à la carte." Indeed, our society's tolerance of do-it-your-
self religion is itself a manifestation of secularization, for in leaving questions of the reality and nature of God or the gods up to
each individual, this attitude implies that there really aren't any
such supernatural entities—or at least implies that we cannot
know, as a society, with any confidence that there are any such
beings. If it were possible to ascertain the existence of, say, a pan-
theon of Greek or Hindu deities or a Jewish or Sikh Supreme Being, then making such a discovery would be of the utmost importance, worthy of the greatest expenditure and exertion. But it

seems obvious that many of our neighbors do not think such a discovery can be made in any intellectually serious and publicly demonstrable way—again, whether they are secularists or religious do-it-yourselfers. All that matters, instead, is whether such beliefs enrich oneself according to one's self-chosen criteria of enrichment without, to reiterate, harming others.

So we encounter the language of public institutions in Canada today, and to a predominant extent also in the United States, whether in politics, news media, entertainment media, or public education. No one, whether a prime minister, a newspaper columnist, a movie hero, or a professor, refers to the Bible as a cultural authority. *Of course* they don't. Even Christians would be not only surprised if someone did but also likely suspicious that such a person was engaged in either manipulation or fanaticism.

The eradication of indubitable authority, however, is much more general than the deposing of the Christian Bible. Again, the point here is not merely the loss of Christian hegemony in North America but basic changes in the very way our neighbors make up their minds about important matters. I join with many others in affirming that the era of debunking we have been living through has produced this final fruit: There is no text, no authority, no canon that anyone can now invoke with the expectation that anyone else, let alone everyone else, will take it seriously, let alone authoritatively. (Compare Peter in the opening text quoting the Jewish Scripture, or Paul on the Areopagus quoting Greek philosophers, as if their listeners were bound to grant the authority of those texts.)

Cultural critic George Steiner testifies to this loss of authority by way of reflections on deconstruction and other postmodern theories of interpretation:

> The relativity, the arbitrariness of *all* aesthetic propositions, of *all* value-judgments is inherent in human consciousness and in human speech. *Anything can be said about anything.* The assertion that Shakespeare's *King Lear* is "beneath serious criticism" (Tolstoy), the finding that Mozart composes mere trivia, are *totally irrefutable*. They can be falsified neither on formal (logical) grounds, nor in existential substance. Aesthetic philosophies, critical theories, constructs of the "classic" or the "canonic" can never be any-

thing but more or less persuasive, more or less comprehensive, more or less consequent descriptions of this or that process of preference. A critical theory, an aesthetic, is a *politics of taste*. . . . No aesthetic proposition can be termed either "right" or "wrong." The sole appropriate response is personal assent or dissent.[2]

What Steiner observes in hermeneutical arcana we can see and hear all around us in popular culture. Sitting in a CBC radio studio recently, I listened while an earnest housewife, with children chatting in the background, read part of the New Testament on the air. While I listened, I watched the host become a little impatient, obviously bemused. My point here is that I believe the host would have responded with the same discomfort to a listener who instead had recited the Qur'an, or read from *The Communist Manifesto*, or quoted Shakespeare, or sung from the Adi Granth, or referred to Plato, or chanted a Native Canadian hymn. To any of these he likely would have replied the way he did to that Christian—with a dismissive "yes, thanks" and then what to him was the real question: "But what does this mean to *you?* How does this *work* in *your* life?"

At the same time, words that formerly possessed particular and substantial religious content are now freely exploited by advertisers and entertainers—even as the echoes of their traditional meanings fade in a culture less and less aware of their primary significance. One walks off a department store escalator in downtown Vancouver through an area devoted to fashionable clothing for youth and steps on floor tiles inscribed with words such as *virgin* and *savior*. One hears all over our culture the word *spirituality* as a term that gives people permission to assert that they are not crass materialists or cold rationalists but something more. That *something*, of course, is defined by themselves, not by any traditional form of spirituality, which by definition is authoritarian and restrictive and thus—ugh—"religious." Lewis Carroll anticipated this attitude:

> "When *I* use a word," Humpty Dumpty [who might have been the original deconstructionist] said, in a rather scornful tone, "it means just what I choose it to mean—neither more nor less."

2. George Steiner, *No Passion Spent* (New Haven/London: Yale University Press, 1996), 25–26.

"The question is," said Alice, "whether you *can* make words mean so many different things."

"The question is," said Humpty Dumpty, "which is to be master—that's all."[3]

In sum, then, we face here a twofold challenge. Our neighbors generally do not know what Christianity really is, even in its most basic form. More troublesome, however, is that many of them increasingly do not think the way Christians do even about how to think about competing versions of truth and virtue. Thus, our conversations never really begin.

Learning to Speak the Languages of Church and Neighbor

At the stroke of midnight on New Year's Day, 1901, at the dawn of the twentieth century, a young woman began to speak in tongues during a watchnight service at Charles Parham's little Bible school in Topeka, Kansas. Soon others joined her, and the Pentecostal movement was born.

The language she spoke was exceedingly unfamiliar. Some later declared it to be Chinese (they did not, it seems, specify the dialect). Now, a midwestern American student might have once heard some German spoken in a movie or learned some French along the way. But to suddenly start speaking in a tongue as foreign as Chinese clearly demonstrated the miraculous power of God.

Encouraged by their reading of Acts 2, some early Pentecostal missionaries set out for the shores of Asia, expecting, upon disembarking, to be enabled miraculously to speak the native languages of other lands. They arrived, however, and could not be understood. Some returned to America discouraged, while others stayed and undertook the arduous work of traditional missionary preparation: language training.[4]

3. Lewis Carroll, *Through the Looking Glass* (New York: Grosset & Dunlap, 1946), 229–30.

4. On the former, see Grant Wacker, "Travail of a Broken Family: Evangelical Responses to Pentecostalism in America, 1906–1916," *Journal of Ecclesiastical History* 47 (July 1996): 517; on the latter, see Gary B. McGee, "Early Pentecostal Hermeneutics: Tongues as Evidence in the Book of Acts," in *Initial Evidence: Historical and Biblical Perspectives on the Pentecostal Doctrine of Spirit Baptism*, ed. Gary B. McGee (Peabody, Mass.: Hendrickson, 1991), 102–3.

The irony here, I submit, is that these ardent Christians were unschooled in their own "language," the tradition of the Christian faith, and so were misled into thinking that God had promised to gift them with another language as well. Instead, it appears that, while Acts 2 does relate that God provided the apostles with a miraculous gift for the debut of the early church, the testimony of Scripture and the historic experience and wisdom of the church over nineteen centuries amounts to this conclusion: God rarely works in this way. Both the church's own language and anyone else's must be acquired the hard way: by living and learning.

First: Speaking the Church's Language

Theologian Brian Hebblethwaite cautions any enthusiastic believer against thinking that he can merely pick up the Bible and proclaim the gospel:

> It is not even possible for us to *mean* what the writers of the Bible and the creeds meant just by saying what they said. We have to embark on the process of interpretation, in the light of our recognition both of their presuppositions and of our own, and struggle to express the truth of God and of God's acts for our own time.[5]

This is the work of theology, and it is work every Christian must do: learning what God has said and learning how to say it for oneself in one's Christian community. The ignorance of the general public about the fundamentals of the Christian faith is regrettable. The ignorance of churchgoing Christians about the fundamentals of the Christian faith, however, is scandalous. Christians are somehow expected to think and feel and live in a distinctive way, as followers of Jesus, without being provided the basic vocabulary, grammar, and concepts of the Christian religion. We can hardly live as Christians if we do not know what "Trinity" or "redemption" means. We can hardly live as Christians if we do not know how to read the laws in Leviticus and the teachings of the Sermon on the Mount. We can hardly live as Christians if we cannot speak the language. And as we

5. Brian Hebblethwaite, *The Incarnation: Collected Essays in Christology* (Cambridge: University of Cambridge Press, 1987), 103.

take a look at the contemporary North American church, we aren't, because we can't.

Would more instruction solve all of our churches' problems? No, of course not. Ideas aren't everything, and theology won't fix everything that is wrong with contemporary Christianity. But *not* being instructed renders us unable to communicate with one another about any other difficulty we might have. As the saying goes, if you think education is expensive, try ignorance.

So the church needs Bible schools and Christian universities; well-trained pastors, Sunday school teachers, and parents; substantial Christian periodicals and books; radio, television, and CD-ROMs; and every other medium to assist us in knowing who we are and what we have to say.

Second: Speaking the Neighbor's Language

The late New Testament scholar F. F. Bruce suggested that it takes seven years to learn another language well, and we all know that the best way to learn a language is by "immersion"— a thorough engagement with the language through reading, carrying on conversations, attending movies, listening to music, transacting business, and just being among other native speakers—as well as by taking formal lessons. As Christians we must ask ourselves, therefore, whether we are taking the steps and paying the price necessary to speak any of the alternative languages, or dialects, of our society today.

Now, acquiring another language does not have to be sheer hard work—as it is, say, for graduate students who are merely satisfying a language requirement for their degrees and have no intrinsic interest in the language itself. Most of us have hobbies or other nonoccupational fascinations. Think of basketball, chamber music, chess, model airplane flying, gardening, or watercolor painting. Each of these pursuits is, in fact, a culture, with its own language, history, conventions, fads, authorities, and values. Part of engaging in such an activity is the acquisition of the language of that culture. It takes time and work but is entirely worthwhile to those who love the craft. The same is true of business, homemaking, or a profession: Entering those activities is like entering another country in which you need to speak the language. To speak the language well means at least understanding the values of that land, if not sharing them—the values that inform the very language everyone uses in it.

We need to bless and commission one another, especially our children and young people, to engage in these kinds of pursuits. We should do so because of their intrinsic value, of course, but we should do so also because we need Christians who are bilingual in this cultural sense, who can readily understand a snowboarder or speak intelligibly and winsomely to a sculptor or a surgeon. We need Christians who can, in a word, speak in those other tongues.

Translating between Them, without Too Much Loss Either Way

Faithful Christian proclamation is not, of course, merely a matter of speaking two languages, as demanding as that is. It is also a matter of translating from one to the other and back again, and therein lies an unhappy paradox today.

On the one hand, the church speaks too *little* the language of the world. I remember hearing a sincere urban pastor exhorting his flock, "We've got to speak the language of the street, folks, or else our ministry won't be a blessing." His last phrase, ironically, would fall on non-evangelical ears as "our X won't be an X."

A so-called seeker-sensitive church recently presented a display advertisement in a Toronto newspaper in order to reach out to its unchurched neighbors. At the bottom of the ad, which featured a list of engaging activities offered by the church, was a slogan guaranteed to constrict the flow of seekers into that sanctuary: "We're a pro-life church!"

A few years ago, another major Canadian newspaper began setting aside space each week on its religion page for a guest column. Anyone in the general public was invited to write. After a few months, the newspaper terminated the experiment. The editors were drowning in screeds from conservative Protestants and Catholics who wanted to condemn godless Canadians for their various sins while wondering plaintively why their wretched neighbors weren't going to church.

On the other hand, too often the church speaks too *much* the language of the world. The Jesuit missionary Matteo Ricci was recalled by the Vatican authorities a few centuries ago because, in their view, he was not merely translating into the native language but was dangerously close to "going native." He was allowing and even incorporating Confucianist rites that his superiors believed were antithetical to authentic Christianity, and he was mistranslating Christian teaching, using Chinese terms drawn from Chinese lore to render Christian terms that, according to Ricci's superiors, could not be adequately translated that way.

Whether or not Ricci was, in the end, correct, his story can alert us to our own difficulties today. American author Rodney Clapp observes:

> Pastors in today's setting are severely tempted to substitute something else for their mother tongue or first language. Perhaps most notably in our context they are tempted to replace theological language with psychological language. Surely psychotherapeutic language has helped many people, Christians included. But it should be the church's second language, not replacing the first language of theology. . . . *Eschatology* is admittedly an awkward . . . term—but is it any less awkward . . . than *dysfunctionality*? Is *redemption* really any less practical or down-to-earth than *self-esteem*?[6]

Furthermore, there is another language vying with psychology for subversive dominance in our churches: the language of the marketplace. I recently spoke with a godly Christian woman with a background in New York City business who was serving on the pastoral search committee of her church. One candidate's lukewarm response to their invitation clearly disappointed her, but I was taken aback when she exclaimed, "He doesn't seem to understand that he's interviewing as a prospective employee." Hmm. Pastors as employees. Attendance figures and donation tallies as markers of success. "Church growth" described as "increase in market share."

The dominance of the psychotherapeutic and the financial are connected, at root, in the consumerist mentality of individual freedom and self-fulfillment. Both are about me and how I can be whom I want and get what I want.

6. Rodney Clapp, *A Peculiar People: The Church as Culture in a Post-Christian Society* (Downers Grove, Ill.: InterVarsity, 1996), 105.

But is the Christian gospel only a promise of health and wealth? Is this all we have to say to the world? As he considers North American Christianity today in its relationship with society at large, pundit Ken Myers reverses the traditional formula and comments sardonically that the church is "of the world, but not in the world."[7]

It is, to be sure, hard, subtle work to translate the gospel and authentic Christian values from our church language into the language of our non-Christian neighbors and to do so without losing too much in the translation. But it is the work to which the Lord of the church calls the church.

Having affirmed that basic imperative, however, we should now consider that other languages appear to have trouble conveying gospel meanings.

Speaking Other Languages Redemptively

It is part of the Christian calling to try to revise our neighbors' view of things, to speak truth in a way that transforms our neighbors' vision. This task will entail, at times, modifying our neighbors' language so that it can more adequately convey what is actually the case.

Let us begin with an apparently quite daunting example of such linguistic reconstruction. What about a language that seems to glorify violence and oppression? What about a language that seems to revel in victory over everyone else? What about the language of—yes—*hockey?*

After being largely removed from Canadian hockey culture for ten years while living in the midwestern United States, I returned to Canada in 1990 to find the revered CBC broadcast *Hockey Night in Canada* featuring an extraordinary person as its main analyst. As a young fan, I had heard Foster Hewitt broadcasting the Maple Leafs' games in Toronto, and Danny Gallivan and Dick Irwin had announced our family's beloved Canadiens "from the Forum in Montreal." But these decent, honorable men had been supplanted by the clownish, thuggish Don Cherry in his "Coaches' Cor-

---

7. Quoted in Ralph C. Wood, "In Defense of Disbelief," *First Things* 88 (October 1998): 30.

ner." Cherry's rendition of hockey glorified Canadian chau-
vinism and anti-European racism; violence, including illegal
and covert mayhem; and manliness defined by playing sto-
ically while injured.

He was talking hockey, but it seemed to me a foreign language. I recognized a fraud when I saw it, because I was raised
in a serious hockey family that was also a serious Christian
family. My grandfather played senior hockey into his fifties.
My dad was good enough to play goal for the Ontario Junior
"A" Peterborough Petes and the Queen's University Golden
Gaels and gave up a shot at making the Montreal Canadiens
only to pursue a career in medicine. Like Don Cherry, my father and grandfather were small town Ontario hockey men,
but unlike Don Cherry, they taught that hockey is primarily
about disciplined skill, artistry, commitment, teamwork, and
fair play. I have very little of my forebears' athletic talent and
experience, but I daresay I understand the game better than
Canada's analyst because my family spoke a different hockey
language, a language deeply influenced by my father's and my
grandfather's Christian commitments. It is not unimportant
here to note furthermore that their understanding of the game
worked. It wasn't just "nice": It was also effective in their
hockey careers. It offered a plausible alternative vision, literally a redemptive definition, as to what was actually "good
hockey."

Can we contest the dominant language of business in the
same way? A Christian friend of mine was studying for an
MBA at a leading American business school. After his first se-
mester, I asked him what the fundamental purpose of a business actually was—having had no background in business my-
self. He rattled off the following proposition as if it were the
great proverb of any sound business: "The primary and over-
riding responsibility of a business is to maximize return to the
shareholders."

One might well be moved to inquire in response, "No matter what the law says? No matter the cost to employees, cus-
tomers, competitors, or innocent bystanders? Is this all a business is for, to make money?" Ebenezer Scrooge and Jacob
Marley succeeded in buying out kind, generous, old Mr. Fez-
ziwig. They were utterly focused on making money and indeed

made lots of it. But Dickens shows us that in the process they lost their souls—and (what is perhaps more interesting at present) the heart of the corporation itself. Christians must join with others to alter the language of the marketplace to include some superior values, to help businesspeople decide afresh what really, literally *counts* in human life, including business life.

And then there is religion. Here is a key example of the need for good translation and yet also of the limits of any such attempt. One can learn what Buddhists mean by "nirvana," even coming to see that Theravada Buddhists mean something quite different by that key term than do Mahayana Buddhists—who in turn disagree among themselves, whether in the various traditions of Zen, Pure Land, Vajrayana, and so on. The Christian can learn what nirvana means and try to relate the Christian teachings of salvation and heaven to it. To communicate the Christian message even in its basic concepts, however, the Christian is going to have to add some terms that simply do not exist in the Buddhist vocabulary: a supreme Being with no other besides; the hope of a "new heaven and new earth" that offer physical as well as spiritual salvation; belief in an everlasting personal identity in communion with everlasting other persons; and so on. Translation, in short, will not finally suffice. Nothing short of linguistic *conversion* will be necessary to communicate fully the Christian message.

The same is true, actually, with our other examples. Don Cherry–type hockey enthusiasts simply lack the vocabulary to understand the alternative mode of defining hockey. Furthermore, if they truly delight in cheating and fighting, then no amount of creative translation will alter their conception of what counts as "good hockey." If businesspeople insist that the bottom line is the only line, then no amount of creative translation will stretch their horizons concerning what counts as "good business." If a person simply does not want to be reconciled to God and acknowledge him as Lord and prefers to inhabit another thought-world, then no amount of creative translation will accommodate these very different understandings of what counts as the "good life."

Incarnating the Message: Body Language

Christians are not, however, limited only to verbal proclamation. Indeed, Christians are called to imitate their Lord in living out the good word of God's truth, a truth that is, after all, directed at transforming all of life.

Out There

Jean de Brébeuf, the seventeenth-century missionary martyr among the Huron Indians of southern Ontario (and one of Canada's patron saints), wrote candidly of the trials of truly incarnational ministry. He warned other would-be missionaries not to follow him to the New World unless they were willing to be truly present with the native people, showing solidarity with them and contextualizing the gospel for them. These are easy words to say, and they have a surprisingly modern, even trendy, sound: "presence," "solidarity," "contextualization." But here is what Brébeuf actually wrote in 1637:

> You must have sincere affection for the Savages [a word that in French, *sauvages*, is not as pejorative as it is in English]—looking upon them as ransomed by the blood of the son of God, and as our Brethren with whom we are to pass the rest of our lives.
>
> To conciliate the Savages, you must be careful never to make them wait for you in embarking. You must provide yourself with a tinder box or with a burning mirror, or with both, to furnish them fire in the daytime to light their pipes, and in the evening when they have to encamp; these little services win their hearts.
>
> You should try to eat their sagamité or salmagundi in the way they prepare it, although it may be dirty, half-cooked, and very tasteless. As to the other numerous things which may be unpleasant, they must be endured for the love of God, without saying anything or appearing to notice them. . . . You must be prompt in embarking and disembarking; and tuck up your gowns so that they will not get wet, and so that you will not carry either water or sand into the canoe. . . .
>
> You must so conduct yourself as not to be at all troublesome to even one of these Barbarians. . . . You must not be ceremonious with the Savages, but accept the comforts they offer you, such as a good place in the cabin. . . .

> Be careful not to annoy anyone in the canoe with your hat; it would be better to take your nightcap.[8]

There is no romance but instead much responsible realism in this advice. Brébeuf and his colleagues so incarnated the gospel that many Hurons were converted, and they so attached themselves to the Hurons that they suffered alongside them in the Iroquois massacre that destroyed their community. This exercise in incarnational translation worked: The Jesuit mission in Huronia was one of the most successful in North American history.

In Here

Hebblethwaite reminds us: "We are not left alone to struggle with the gap between our words and the divine reality. God comes to meet us where we are in the incarnate Word."[9] Nor has God left us to struggle with the gap between the words of Scripture *about* the incarnate Word and our reception of them. He bridges that gap by the personal presence of the Holy Spirit, who interprets Scripture to us within our hearts, and by the mutual instruction and manifestation of truth within the body of Christ, the church.

The church's most vivid articulation of the gospel, and its most cogent defense of the gospel, is not argument in its sermons and books but *depiction* in its worship, fellowship, and ministry to the world. The kingdom of God, after all, is like a mustard seed, a field, and a housewife—but it is especially like the church. The kingdom of God is within you. Therefore, Jesus said, "Let your light shine before others, so that they may see your good works and give glory to your Father in heaven" (Matt. 5:16 NRSV).

Trusting God for Communication and Its Results

Nisi dominus frustra happens to be the Stackhouse family motto, as it is of other, much more remarkable, families (in-

---

8. Jean de Brébeuf, "Instructions for the Fathers of Our Society Who Shall Be Sent to the Hurons," in *The Jesuit Relations and Allied Documents: A Selection,* ed. S. R. Mealing (Toronto/Montreal: McClelland and Stewart, 1963), 48–49.

9. Hebblethwaite, *Incarnation,* 152.

cluding the Dutch royal House of Orange). It is a version of the
opening of Psalm 127 and expresses a basic truth to which we
need to return in this matter of communication. "Without the
Lord, frustration"; "It is in vain without the Lord"; or, from a
typical English translation, "Unless the Lord builds the house,
they labor in vain who build it."

The three themes of communication, frustration, and God
have a long history. The primeval story of Babel shows an apparently happier time in which everyone understood everyone
else because they spoke the same language. But understanding,
it seems, does not necessarily lead to goodness.

> Then they said, "Come, let us build ourselves a city, and a tower
> with its top in the heavens, and let us make a name for ourselves;
> otherwise we shall be scattered abroad upon the face of the
> whole earth." The Lord came down to see the city and the tower,
> which mortals had built. And the Lord said, "Look, they are one
> people, and they have all one language; and this is only the be-
> ginning of what they will do; nothing that they propose to do will
> now be impossible for them. Come, let us go down, and confuse
> [frustrate] their language there, so that they will not understand
> one another's speech." So the Lord scattered them abroad from
> there over the face of all the earth, and they left off building the
> city. Therefore it was called Babel, because there the Lord con-
> fused [frustrated] the language of all the earth; and from there
> the Lord scattered them abroad over the face of all the earth.
>
> Genesis 11:4–9 NRSV

This story includes many mysteries, most of which we cannot pause to consider here. But we can see, as we consider it in
the light of the text from the Book of Acts about Pentecost, two
crucial aspects of our theme.

First, what God put asunder at Babel he began to join together at Pentecost. God intends the peoples of the earth once
more to understand one another, but now in the common
project of building and inhabiting the New Jerusalem, not the
ancient tower of Babel. Thus, those of us who attempt to learn
and speak the language of our neighbors, however foreign it
may be and however difficult to learn, can be assured of the
blessing of God in that task. Despite the splintering of humanity
into self-enclosed, self-absorbed individuals and communities—

as is advocated nowadays both by genocidal politicians and radical postmodern theorists—God's great project is to reunite us, to help us communicate across barriers of race, sex, religion, class, and all other impediments including, at base, the barrier of language.

Second, it is God alone who grants the gift of language and the gift of true communication. Even if God were to let each Christian suddenly begin to speak the gospel in another tongue, there is no guarantee that the rest of us would welcome it. Even on that great Pentecost—*especially* on that Pentecost—some heard what was said and profited from it while others mocked the message as drunken gibberish. Thus will the gospel come across to some as the word of life and yet to others as the incomprehensible ravings of the spiritually intoxicated. And we Christians cannot help that. It is not a matter of linguistic ability or inability on our part but of spiritual interest on theirs. Any substantial, true communication is a gift of God—a gift that human beings have the awful privilege of rejecting.

Conclusion: "A Time to Keep Silence, a Time to Speak"

We should acknowledge finally that sometimes silence is our most appropriate response to our neighbor. Sometimes we need not to speak but only to listen, or to wait. Evangelical Christians, inclined to be verbal and even verbose, sometimes need to be quiet and work alongside others on the priority of the moment.

Brébeuf gave good counsel, perhaps surprising counsel, in this respect also:

> It is well not to ask many questions, nor should you yield to your desire to learn the language and to make observations on the way; this may be carried too far. You must relieve those in your canoe of this annoyance, especially as you cannot profit much by it during the work. Silence is a good equipment at such a time.[10]

10. Brébeuf, "Instructions for the Fathers," 49.

Sometimes, too, Christians must attend to matters given to them by God that are not viewed as important, or even good, by others. We speak our own language, according to the logic of God's country, and that can include spending time and money and words and talent on apparently bizarre pursuits—such as receiving communion in church, memorizing Scripture, or teaching children Bible stories.

At some extreme point—alas!—we may have to keep silence in another, horrible way, as we abandon some of our neighbors, at least for a time, to their chosen paths. Christ himself finally stopped answering his opponents' questions in his last days, and there may come a time—for some of us as individuals or even for certain churches in certain societies—when Christians will have to maintain silence as a rebuke to the world's misguided agendas.

Until that time comes, however—and I daresay it has not come for most of us—let every Christian proclaim the gospel as best he or she can, with eloquence of word and deed matched as nicely as possible to the needs of our neighbors. May each of us who follow the apostolic band, our heroes at Pentecost, speak well in tongues.

Index